T0051755

25ᵀᴴ ANNIVERSARY EDITION

AUTISM

— AND —

DIFFICULT
MOMENTS

Practical Solutions for
Reducing Meltdowns

BRENDA SMITH MYLES, PhD

Advance Praise for
AUTISM AND DIFFICULT MOMENTS

What autistic people who have a meltdown need is people around them who look beyond their behavior, people who see autistic people first and foremost as human beings, with the same needs and wants as all other people, but with a brain that ensures that the world is much more threatening. People who don't see them and their behavior as difficult, but who are willing to understand and support. Brenda Myles succeeds (again) in writing a book with a wealth of practical and useful strategies. She shows a deep human understanding of how autistic people struggle with the world and how we can support them when things get too much. Anyone who wants to show an empathetic and compassionate response to autistic people having a meltdown should read this book.

> — Peter Vermeulen, author of *Autism as Context Blindness* and *Autism and the Predictive Brain: Absolute Thinking in a Relative World*

I'm delighted to see a new edition of this valuable and important book. Written in Brenda's clear, precise and unambiguous style, this an accessible resource for individuals, families and professionals. I know my thinking and practice will be improved from reading, studying and referring to it. Be careful who you loan this to as, in my experience, it is the sort of book that is rarely returned …

> — Jim Taylor, award-winning speaker and consultant, Scotland UK

Brenda's book provides an understanding of why behaviors of concern occur and the role support personnel play in meltdowns and difficult moments. Understanding autistic neurology, knowing the meltdown cycle, and assessing behavior by going beyond what we see gives us greater insight into difficulties that may appear like they've come out of nowhere. Brenda provides respectful, thoughtful teaching tools and resources to help support personnel have a deeper understanding of the "why" of autistic behavior and to assist in guiding autistic individuals to better understand themselves and achieve well-being.

> — Maureen Bennie, director, Autism Awareness Centre Inc.

Brenda Smith Myles brings new life to a classic! Full of the latest research, case studies and strategies, Myles gives a user friendly voice to understanding behaviors and autism. It was the first book on my shelf 20 years ago and it's even better now. A must have for every parent, teacher and therapist —BRAVO!

— Sherry A. Moyer, LMSW

If you are seeking to provide compassionate support to an autistic client, student or loved one, Autism and Difficult Moments: Practical Solutions for Meltdowns is for you. Brenda Smith Myles breaks down the autistic neurology and meltdown cycle in a simple, easy to digest format and provides lots of practical ideas for promoting regulation. I highly recommend this book!

— Kelly Mahler OTD, OTR/L, author of *The Interoception Curriculum: A Step-by-Step Guide to Developing Mindful Self-Regulation*

As an individual who has ASD I really appreciate all of the strategies that Myles provides in this book for helping support people better understand and help those who have Autism. I think that it is very beneficial that Interoception is mentioned in this edition of the book as it is something that affects me and many others with ASD. I frequently went from 0-100 without realizing it, and was often referred to as attention seeking and manipulative before I worked on my interoception awareness skills and was better understood and supported by individuals in my environment.

— Chloe Rothschild, autistic advocate and speaker

AUTISM AND DIFFICULT MOMENTS:
Practical Solutions for Reducing Meltdowns

All marketing and publishing rights guaranteed to and reserved by:

FUTURE HORIZONS

(817) 277-0727

(817) 277-2270 (fax)

E-mail: info@fhautism.com

www.fhautism.com

ISBN: 9781957984322

CONTENTS

CHAPTER 3

Overview of Functional Behavior Assessment 45

CHAPTER 4

Strategies That Promote Regulation 59

Contents

CHAPTER 1

Characteristics of Autism— Neurological Research Findings

B y now, almost everyone who has lived with, worked with, befriended, or supported an autistic person or who is autistic realizes that the behaviors that we consider to be "autistic"—such as flapping, repeating words or sentences, flinching around loud noises, and focusing on a topic for a long time— are strategies used to cope with a world that can be unfriendly and overwhelming. And often, these strategies are the only ones the autistic person has available in a given situation. In addition, thanks to current research in autism, which is dominated by neurological studies, we have come to understand that "autistic behaviors" are brain-based.

This brief chapter will review some of the neurological research on autism and its connection—directly and indirectly— to meltdowns. This is in no way meant to be a comprehensive review of the literature on the autistic neurology. The aim of this chapter is to allow readers to see the relationships between neurology and behaviors in autism with a focus on practical applications and, specifically, to prevent those who support autistic individuals from mistakenly thinking that meltdowns are "purposeful behavior" and that unique responses to interventions are "willful disobedience."

Self-Regulation and the Brain

The ability to self-regulate is neurological (Ni et al., 2020). Richey and colleagues (2015) found less activity in the parts of the brain that regulate emotions of autistic people than in the neuromajority.[1] Challenges in regulation are brain-based—not purposeful behavior (Phung, 2021)!

Lewis and Stevens' interviews of autistic adults confirm this. They reported,

> During a meltdown, we found that most autistics described feeling overwhelmed by information, senses, and social and emotional stress. They often felt extreme emotions, such as anger, sadness, and fear, and had trouble with thinking and memory during the meltdown. Participants described trying to stay in control of themselves, often feeling like they were not themselves during meltdowns. They described the meltdown as a way of letting go of or releasing the extreme emotions they felt. Participants tried to stay away from things or people that might trigger a meltdown or tried to make sure they were alone if they felt a meltdown may be coming as a way of avoiding harm—including harm to their bodies, their emotions, and their relationships (2023, p. 1).

---

1. The term "neuromajority" is used throughout this book instead of the often-used term "neurotypical" as there is nothing typical about people known as neurotypicals. There just seems to be more of them—hence the term "neuromajority." Thanks to Judy Endow for sharing this wisdom with me.

Judy Endow:

When I am not well regulated, I am less able to engage in what is going on around me. It takes me much longer to process my thoughts. And, thus, my reaction time to the spoken words of others is much slower, and my reactions to extraneous stimuli become bigger and louder and last longer. I am told that my voice becomes louder and that I have a startle response to stimuli that normally would not cause me to startle. Until science advances enough to enable us to better understand and impact our neurological movement glitches—physical, thinking, and emotional fluidity—many of us with autism can learn to proactively outsmart at least some of the movement difficulties we experience by addressing our regulation needs.

(Retrieved from www.judyendow.com)

Lisa D:

Unlike temper tantrums, meltdowns are not manipulative tactics. Handling and preventing meltdowns is an important autistic life skill; and learning to predict them is a prerequisite to learning to prevent them. As we all probably already know, it's impossible to stop a meltdown once it happens—thus the focus on prevention.

(Retrieved from www.judyendow.com)

Leigh:

Many autistic people are said to have difficulty understanding, labeling, and describing their feelings, but I've always considered myself to be quite lucky in this respect—I've always thought I could describe how I felt, most of the time at least. So, when Joanna (my co-admin on this site) asked me yesterday, "How do you know when you're happy," I blithely answered, "When

I'm feeling cheerful ... when I have that joie de vivre, that glow inside. When I'm glad to be alive." "Yes," she said. "But how does that actually feel?" And I was stumped. She explained that I'd answered a question about a feeling by just using other feelings to describe it, leaving her no wiser about my experience of happiness.

(Retrieved from www.judyendow.com)

Sensory Issues and the Brain

What do all of these (Family Doctor, 2023) have in common?
- Think clothing feels too scratchy or itchy
- Think lights seem too bright
- Think sounds seem too loud
- Think soft touches feel too hard
- Gag when experiencing food textures
- Have poor balance or seem clumsy
- Are afraid to play on the swings
- React poorly to sudden movements, touches, loud noises, or bright lights
- Have behavior problems
- Seek thrills (loves jumping heights, and spinning
- Can't spin without getting dizzy
- Don't pick up on social cues
- Don't recognize personal space
- Chew on things (including their hands and clothing)
- Seek visual stimulation (like electronics)
- Have problems sleeping
- Don't recognize when their face is dirty or nose is running

These are all behaviors that are sensory-based; behaviors that are challenging for autistic individuals; and behaviors that can impact the everyday experiences of autistics. In short, they are barriers to achieving limitless potential (Lee Stickle, personal communication, July 2015).

The Senses

Neurological research confirms that the autistic brain perceives sensory input differently than neuromajority brains. For example, studies have reported challenges in the sensory systems related to the auditory (Green et al., 2015; Rotschafer, 2021), tactile (Espenhahn, 2022; Green et al., 2015), proprioceptive (Armitano-Lago, 2021; Marko et al., 2015), and visual senses (Chung, 2020; Soulières et al., 2009), with the visual system touted as a strength. In addition, behavioral differences have been identified in the olfactory and gustatory senses (Boudiarane, 2017). Further, the "overload of sensations" reported by many autistic adults (see below) has been supported in the neurological research (Green et al., 2015; Rowland, 2020). However, some autistics experience the opposite; that is, they fail to process certain sensations (Kilroy et al., 2019). Table 1.1 provides an overview of the sensory systems.

Table 1.1. Location and Functions of the Sensory Systems

System	Location	Function
Tactile *(touch)*	Skin – density of cell distribution varies throughout the body. Areas of greatest density include mouth, hands, and genitals.	Provides information about the environment and object qualities (touch, pressure, texture, hard, soft, sharp, dull, heat, cold, pain).
Vestibular *(balance)*	Inner ear – stimulated by head movements and input from other senses, especially visual.	Provides information about where our body is in space, and whether or not we or our surroundings are moving. Tells about speed and direction of movement.
Proprioception *(body awareness)*	Muscles and joints – activated by muscle contractions and movement.	Provides information about where a certain body part is and how it is moving.
Visual *(sight)*	Retina of the eye – stimulated by light.	Provides information about objects and persons. Helps us define boundaries as we move through time and space.
Auditory *(hearing)*	Inner ear – stimulated by air/sound waves.	Provides information about sounds in the environment (loud, soft, high, low, near, far).
Gustatory *(taste)*	Chemical receptors in the tongue – closely entwined with the olfactory (smell) system.	Provides information about different types of taste (sweet, sour, bitter, salty, spicy).
Olfactory *(smell)*	Chemical receptors in the nasal structure – closely associated with the gustatory system.	Provides information about different types of smell (musty, acrid, putrid, flowery, pungent).
Interoception *(inside body)*	Inside of your body – helps the body "feel" the internal state or conditions of the body.	Provides information such as pain, body temperature, itch, sexual arousal, hunger and thirst. It also helps bring in information regarding heart and breathing rates and when we need to use the bathroom.

With sincere gratitude and apologies to Kelly Mahler

More about Interoception

The little-known but extremely important sensory system called interoception helps us to "feel" our internal state or conditions of our body. The interoceptive system brings in information such as pain, body temperature, itch, sexual arousal, hunger, and thirst. It also helps bring in information regarding heart and breathing rates and when we need to use the bathroom.

Approximately 85 percent of autistic people have difficulty identifying and understanding their emotions. They may not receive the signals necessary for this to occur or may confuse one emotion for another (e.g., mistake hunger for anger). In school, interoceptive challenges—not understanding how you are feeling—impact "a student's success in regulating classroom behaviors, such as their ability to attend to classroom activities, participate in group assignments, solve problems, complete schoolwork, and feel safe in their learning environments" (Mahler et al., 2022, pg. 2).

Most importantly, in the context of this book, the interoception system lets individuals know when they are irritated, overwhelmed, upset, or anxious—all of which are related to potential meltdowns.

If a person does not effectively receive or interpret signals regarding how they are feeling, it is almost impossible for them to take action to self-regulate. Even if the autistic individual knows strategies to calm down, this information is useless unless they know that they are becoming upset (Mahler, 2019).

Clearly, there are many complexities that remain to be understood, but in this context, one thing is clear: being overwhelmed by sensory input (e.g., sound, taste, smells) or being unaware of sensory stimuli in the environment can result in meltdowns.

Sophie:

When I get sensory overload, it is like I have 100 buzzy bees in my head, and my head hurts a lot and feels like it will go "bang" like a balloon. It is the most uncomfortable thing ever!!! I have to try to bang my head on things to try to relieve the pressure in my head to stop the feeling. While I am experiencing sensory overload, I find it very hard to talk or make any sentences, as my speech just won't come out as I want it too, and I can't make the words make sense.

(Retrieved from https://www.autismspeaks.org/blog/2015/01/21/ nonverbal-adult-shares-her-feelings-sensory-overload)

Bessel:

Agency starts with what scientists call interoception, our awareness of our subtle sensory, body-based feelings: the greater that awareness, the greater our potential to control our lives.

(Retrieved from https://quotefancy.com/quote/2569403/Bessel-A-van-der-Kolk-Agency- starts-with-what-scientists-call-interoception-our-awareness)

Megan:

Once I learned about the connection between interoception and autism, I gained a better understanding of why my body has often felt confusing to occupy.

(Retrieved from https://neurodivergentinsights.com/blog/autism-interoception)

Reinforcement and the Brain

Comparing the response to social and monetary rewards in the brains of autistic individuals to those of neuromajority individuals, Baumeister et al. (2023) found a difference between the two groups with respect to both types of rewards. Specifically, in autistic individuals, the reward center of the brain, known as the mesocorticolimbic reward center, was underactive.

These brain-based differences may mean that situations that provide adequate reinforcers meant for the neuromajority do not provide adequate reinforcement for autistics. It is easy to see how a lack of positive reinforcement for appropriate behavior might lead to the frustration and anxiety that set the meltdown cycle into motion.

Chloe:

Positive reinforcement is important to me as a young autistic adult. I work so hard each and every single day, trying my best and giving it my all. Even if my progress and milestones may be small or different than others', they still deserve to be noticed. Something like asking to take a break isn't easy for me to do, so when I do, praise and positive words of encouragement are helpful. I want my efforts to be noticed.

(Personal communication with Chloe Rothschild, October 19, 2015)

BF Skinner:

"What is love except another name for the use of positive reinforcement? Or vice versa."

(Retrieved from https://www.facebook.com/watch/?v=323044961944806)

Prediction and the Brain

With sincere gratitude and apologies to Peter Vermeulen.

Imagine not being able to predict what is going to happen next. What would you do? Most likely you would:

- Cling to the activities and events that are familiar
- Not willingly try new ventures
- Experience anxiety and/or behavior challenges when you are *merely introduced to the possibility* of participating in new events or activities
- Protest, refuse, or meltdown when forced to engage in a new activity or event
- Feel overwhelmed by the possibility of the actuality of a change

How important is prediction in daily life? Research suggests that even *before* activities and events occur, people know or can largely estimate what is likely to happen. This is known as external chance. They also estimate their chance of success even before they attempt an activity or event—this is called internal chance. The ability to predict guides us toward tasks and problems we are likely to solve and steers us way from those that might be too difficult.

Peter Vermeulen (2023), in his book *Autism and the Predictive Brain: Absolute Thinking in a Relative World*, shares that prediction is neurologically based. He explains that the way people experience the world comes from within. Neuromajority brains sense in advance what they will see, hear, touch, smell, taste and feel. In fact, the brain actually creates a model of what is expected. The autistic neurology, however, does not know how to predict.

Autistic people experience challenges in knowing what will happen next; they cannot anticipate how they are to react and do not have a sense that they will be successful. Indeed, they anticipate the opposite: confusion and failure.

Sinha et al. (2014), shares this quote about prediction, equating it to magic,

> An essential component of a magical phenomenon is the lack of a discernible cause: An event that we are unable to predict happens "as if by magic." Given how well-honed our predictive abilities are, magicians have to resort to clever contrivances to achieve their mystifying effects. However, if our predictive abilities were somehow to be compromised, then even mundane occurrences in the environment might appear magical. Although a brief magical performance is enjoyable, unrelenting immersion in it can be overwhelming. A magical world suggests lack of control and impairs one's ability to take preparatory actions (p. 15220).

An inability to predict means that the autistic individual cannot prepare for upcoming events and activities and feels as if they have no control over their environment. In the above, substitute the word "terror" for "magical," and we might begin to understand why autistic people cling to sameness, do not like change, and consider surprises as negative. It explains why many autistics experience meltdowns.

Lyric:

I fit the autism stereotype of being an Autistic Person who does not handle change well; and in that sense, I mean, I am someone who can have meltdowns and shutdowns, if a surprise change happens to me. So my reaction to not handling change well is often apparent to other people, and it has been something that I have dealt with my entire life.

(Retrieved from https://neurodivergentrebel.com/2022/01/19/autism-change-why-change-is-hard-for-me-as-an-autistic-person/)

Context and the Brain

With sincere gratitude and apologies to Peter Vermeulen

According to dictionary.com, *context* is the conditions and circumstances that are relevant to an event, fact, etc. How we interpret the world around us depends on context. For example, context helps us quickly recognize and identify situations and things in our environment and helps us to understand what is relevant. Context also provides predictability: It tells us what to expect.

In his review of neurological research and context for autistic individuals, Vermeulen (2012) pointed out that everything is sensitive to context. "Nothing in the world has an absolute meaning. A bag of garbage is not always a bag of garbage. Sometimes it is art" (p. 16). How we interpret our boss' message depends on the situation; how we understand our mother's facial expression depends on the situation. Everything is based on context—emotion recognition, the perceptions of others, our statements and questions, and overall behavior.

For most people, context "just is." Neuromajority individuals automatically interpret context—usually within 200 milliseconds. In contrast, autistic individuals often must assemble situations and contexts in order to make sense of them (Vermeulen, 2012).

In the documentary film *Automatically*, Michelle tells how she recognizes her living room. Contrary to people without autism, Michelle does not recognize her living room in the blink of an eye. She first sees totally separate things: a flower, a VCR, a TV, a figurine on the mantle, the CD rack, and so on. Only when she makes a conscious effort does she succeed in assembling all of these impressions into a living room. Michelle also immediately notices when something has changed in her living room, even if it is only a slight detail (Vermeulen, 2012, 57).

According to Vermeulen (2012), autistic people "have a keen eye for details, but not for all details. They excel in details for which context does not play a role" (p. 101). This means that they must expend considerable energy on first identifying objects, situations, people, and so forth in their environment in a rote manner, and then, *if they have been taught how to understand context*, attempt to make the information meaningful. For autistics, this is a deliberate process. For those without autism, this is a split-second automatic task. How exhausting this must be for an autistic person! And can this lead to meltdowns? Yes!

How else does context relate to meltdowns? Interpretation without context can lead to misunderstandings, error, and frustration. Context blindness can lead to heightened stress and anxiety because of the likely occurrence of mistakes in understanding social interactions. Difficulties with understanding context can also lead to an overreliance on predictability. Once an autistic individual has interpreted one situation correctly, he tends to rely on that interpretation in other events even if the context is different.

Dora:

The experience of many of us is not that 'insistence on sameness' jumps out unbidden and unwanted and makes our lives hard, but that 'insistence on sameness' is actually a way of adapting to a confusing and chaotic environment.

(Retrieved from https://the-art-of-autism.com/ favorite-quotes-about-autism-and-aspergers/)

Jeannie Davide-Rivera:

A child [with autism] … will only understand the stove is hot after touching it, or being burned. This child does not, however, apply this newfound knowledge to the toast being hot, or other items that are intuitively drawn from the realization of what "hot" means. … The relative concepts of things that are hot are not generalized over a wide range of contexts.

(Retrieved from: http://aspiewriter.com/2014/08/autism-and-central-coherence-missing-the-forest-for-the-trees.html)

Catatonia and the Brain

With sincere gratitude and apologies to Ruth Aspy

Catatonia is a brain-based disorder of posture/movement, speech, mood, and behavior (Ghaziuddin et al., 2021). The latest edition of the *Diagnostic and Statistical Manual of Mental Disorders* (5th ed., American Psychiatric Association, 2013; DSM-5) includes catatonia as a specifier for autism. Indeed, approximately 20 percent of young autistic people demonstrate some symptoms of catatonia (Vaquerizo-Serrano et al., 2022).

Catatonia has many complex (and confusing) presentations. Some overlap with the underlying characteristics of autism. When catatonia is present in an autistic person, they may have difficulty starting a motion, such as following directions or drinking when thirsty. They may also have difficulty stopping a motion. They may kick or hit someone when it is actually the opposite of what they intended to do.

The presence of catatonia is stressful and confusing both for autistic people and those in their environment. Clearly, such stress along with the characteristics of catatonia and movement challenges increases the risk of meltdowns.

Judy:

When I am not well regulated, I also have significantly more movement issues. I must bring conscious thought to my physical movement, such as walking, grasping, and chewing. It becomes difficult to engage in multiple movements at the same time, such as walking over to a person and handing him something. First, I have to walk over to the person, stop, and then execute the handing-something motion. It also becomes difficult to combine physical movement with thinking. This means that I have to stop moving in order to think any thoughts unrelated to the actual act of moving my body through space. As a result, it is nearly impossible for me to walk and talk at the same time.

(Retrieved from http://www.judyendow.com/autistic-behavior/autism-sensory-regulation-and-movement-fluidity/)

Devon:

Research shows that most Autistic people have a reduced sense of the body's warning signals, or interoception. Most of us tend to feel like our bodies are not really our own, and struggle to draw connections between the external world and how we feel inside.

(Retrieved from https://www.goodreads.com/work/quotes/91968379-unmasking-autism-discovering-the-new-faces-of-neurodiversity)

Summary

We are still in the genesis of understanding autism. In recent years, brain-based research and the perspectives of autistic individuals themselves have greatly contributed to our understanding, especially in the areas of meltdowns and other issues of regulation. Knowledge of the neurological underpinnings of autism may lead to more patient and therapeutic responses to difficulties with regulation and a decreased tendency to respond in a punitive or judgmental manner.

CHAPTER 2

The
Meltdown
Cycle

We all experience stress. Most of the time, our stress is minor and/or easily addressed. However, many autistic individuals experience stress that is ongoing and of greater magnitude. And as a result, their stress can be debilitating.

Common stressors include:

- Sensory issues (e.g., loud sounds, sudden sounds, odors, lighting, bright colors, patterns, moving objects)
- Lack of predictability
- Difficulty communicating wants, needs, or ideas
- Changes in events, including being added, canceled, resequenced, shortened, lengthened
- Perfectionism/fear of making mistakes
- Losing a game
- Being unable to convince others that your way is the correct way
- Being timed on tasks
- Facing unresolved problems
- Breaking a rule
- Anticipation of any events that will negatively impact you (e.g., negative feedback, failing to meet a standard, disappointing someone)
- Being mistreated or treated unkindly (e.g., sarcasm, bullying, being left out of an activity)

In addition to generally experiencing more frequent and more severe stress than others, when they are first becoming stressed, autistic people often do not indicate in ways that are meaningful to others that they are under stress or having difficulty coping. In fact, they themselves do not always know that they are near a stage of crisis. Quite often they just "tune out" or daydream, pace, laugh, or state in a monotone voice a seemingly benign phrase, such as "I don't know what to do." Since limited or no traditional expressions of emotion may be conveyed, these signs of stress often go unnoticed by others in the environment.

Therefore, when at a later point in time, the autistic individual engages in a verbally or physically "aggressive" event or shuts down, it seems to happen without provocation. This is often called a meltdown. The person may begin to scream, kick over a piece of furniture, or totally shut down. For those who are not familiar with the characteristics of autism, there seems to be no predictability to this behavior; it just occurs.

Sometimes support personnel report that an autistic individual is doing fine or managing at school or work. However, family members report that when she arrives home, she loses control. That is, she experiences a meltdown. It seems that many autistic people use all their self-control to manage at school or work and that once they get to a safe environment (e.g., home), they let go of some of the pressure that is bottled up within them. Thus, the meltdown can occur in a totally different place from where the stressor was originally encountered.

But although it may seem that way, meltdowns do not occur without warning! Rather, autistic individuals exhibit a pattern of behaviors that are precursors to a meltdown. Sometimes these behaviors are subtle. In fact, those who do not know the person often report that a meltdown comes "out of nowhere." One teacher reported, "Susan was just sitting at her desk quietly. The next thing I know, she had a meltdown. She totally lost control, overturned her desk, and began flailing her arms. I had no warning."

Without training and/or experience—that is, without knowing the connections between meltdowns and autism—the neuromajority person observing a meltdown may draw uncharitable conclusions. As a result, meltdown behaviors may result in rejection, punishment, fear, or judgment.

The alternative perspective presented here will lead to more preventive strategies being put in place and more supportive responses given when meltdowns occur. **This is the kind alternative to uncompassionate misperceptions and misguided responses.**

Without a clear understanding of meltdowns and the cycle by which they occur, one may indeed think that meltdowns occur without warning. This chapter explains the cycle of meltdowns and how it affects both autistic individuals and others in their environment. For each stage, behaviors and interventions are outlined, including suggestions for when the individual is ready to learn.

The Cycle of Meltdowns

Because meltdowns occur for a reason, it is important to understand the underlying causes or antecedent—that is, the triggers. The cycle typically runs through three stages: **Rumbling**, **Rage**, and **Recovery** (adapted from Albert, 1989; Beck, 1985). These stages may be of variable length, with one stage lasting hours and another only a few minutes.

It is important to understand the following regarding the Cycle of Meltdowns:

- The cycle occurs for a reason.
- Each episode is preceded by a reason or reasons
- The build-up to a meltdown is typically manifested in the same way across episodes.
- Recovery may or may not look the same after each meltdown.
- The autistic individual cannot learn new skills during the cycle.

The three stages of the cycle, illustrated in Figure 2.1, show the cycle that the autistic individual progresses through when having a meltdown. It should be noted, however, that the cycle is also experienced—in a lesser degree—by the support person. Most people focus on the cycle experienced by the autistic, and rightfully so. However, the stress experienced by the support person is a part of the interaction and must be addressed as well. It is the responsibility of the adult to maintain a presentation of calmness throughout the cycle, even if they feel emotionally distraught.

Figure 2.1. Cycle Of Meltdowns

Note the "ready to learn" segments in Figure 2.1. These are the ONLY times when the autistic person is available to learn new skills. When they are in the Rumbling, Rage, or Recovery Stage, they cannot learn new skills but can only use skills that they already know and are able to use fluently.

Learning can only occur when we are well-regulated! The No Learning Zone in Figure 2.1 clearly shows that no learning can occur during the Cycle of Meltdowns. This is important to recognize and respect. Failure to do so may escalate and prolong the cycle and cause additional frustration for both the individual with autism and the support person. Remember, the autistic individual is not choosing not to learn during the cycle—this is the way the autistic neurology functions.

Also, note the arrows attached to the Rumbling and Rage stages. If an adult can effectively recognize and support the individual during these two stages, the learner can be ready to learn. There is no such exit during the Rage Stage. Once the individual is in the Rage Stage, they *must* go through the Recovery Stage in order to be ready to learn.

Does verbal de-escalation work? Many of us have been taught that "talking someone down" when someone is experiencing the Cycle of Meltdowns is effective. Known as verbal de-escalation, this strategy has some support for the neuromajority. For autistic individuals, extensive verbalizations may have the opposite effect (see Figure 2.2). If you attempt to "talk the individual down," they may not be able to process what is being said. This, in turn, could escalate the Cycle of Meltdowns. It is best to limit verbalizations during the cycle.

Figure 2.2. Unintended Impact of Verbalizations by
a Support Person During a Meltdown

Retrieved from https://www.autismdailynewscast.com/autism-hyperacusis-torment-sound//

In the following, we will look at each of the three stages and present interventions that have been found to be effective for each.

The Rumbling Stage

The first stage in the cycle is the Rumbling Stage. The goal during this stage is to distract and calm the individual. Remember: the behavior is not purposeful; it is neurologically based. Rumbling behaviors occur because the autistic individual has not been effectively taught (a) skills to recognize how they feel or (b) skills to remain calm (see Figure 2.3).

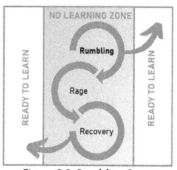

Figure 2.3. Rumbling Stage

"Behaviors" of the Individual

During the Rumbling Stage, autistic individuals exhibit specific behavioral changes that may not appear to be directly related to a meltdown. They may bite their nails or lips, lower their voices, tense their muscles, tap their foot, grimace, or otherwise indicate general discontent. In addition, they may appear to be slightly off-task, disengaged, or "off the mark." They may complain of not feeling well. It is easy for others to ignore these seemingly minor behaviors, yet they often signal an impending crisis.

In other instances, autistic individuals engage in behaviors that are more pronounced, including withdrawing from others, either emotionally or physically; threatening others, either verbally or physically; or questioning the rules or authority.

Support Person Behaviors

As the autistic person's behavior escalates, the support person's behavior usually follows. Thus, those in a support role must realize that they may be experiencing their own rumbling behaviors along with the autistic individual. It is the responsibility of the support person to remain or project the image of calmness. If the support person does not, the behavior of the autistic individual is likely to escalate.

Regardless of the specific intervention selected, certain general approaches are helpful when seeking to help the person who is rumbling. During this stage, it is imperative that the support person remains calm and uses a quiet voice so he or she can focus on helping the individual move toward a more regulated state. It is almost impossible for the autistic person to be flexible unless he has been taught flexibility and it is firmly entrenched in his repertoire.

During this stage, the support person must be kind, reevaluate the goals, and be flexible so that the autistic individual can meet the "new" goal: **to get back to the where the individual can learn.** The following behaviors are typically effective for those supporting an autistic individual at this stage:

- Remain calm.
- Use a quiet voice.
- Take deep breaths.
- Reevaluate student goals.
- Be flexible—the autistic individual is not able to be once the Cycle of Meltdowns has begun.

Just as it is important to understand support person behavior that may diffuse a crisis, it is important to recognize which support person behaviors are likely to result in an escalation. The behaviors listed in Table 2.1 are almost certain to turn a potential crisis into a meltdown (Albert, 1989).

Table 2.1. Support Person Behaviors That Can Escalate a Crisis

- Raising voice or yelling
- Making assumptions
- Preaching
- Backing the student into a corner
- Saying, "I'm the boss here"
- Pleading or bribing
- Insisting on having the last word
- Bringing up unrelated events

- Using tense body language
- Generalizing by making remarks such as "You guys are all the same"
- Being sarcastic
- Attacking the individual's character
- Making unsubstantiated accusations
- Nagging
- Holding a grudge
- Acting superior
- Throwing a temper tantrum
- Using unwarranted physical force
- Mimicking the individual
- Drawing unrelated persons into the conflict
- Making comparisons with the behavior of other people, etc.
- Insisting on being right
- Having a double standard: "Do what I say, not what I do"
- Commanding, demanding, dominating
- Rewarding the individual for unacceptable behavior
- Using degrading, insulting, humiliating, or embarrassing putdowns

Interventions

During the Rumbling Stage, it is imperative that the support person intervenes without becoming part of a struggle. Because many autistics do not recognize that they are under stress or are experiencing discomfort associated with the rumbling state (Mahler et al., 2022), the help and insight of a support person can make the difference between escalation and resolution of a challenging experience.

Many effective interventions during this stage fall in the category of **surface behavior management** (Long, Morse, & Newman, 1976). This includes strategies such as antiseptic bouncing, proximity control, signal interference, and touch control. Strategies that do not fall under the category of surface management may also be used—strategies that are therapeutic, not punitive, and designed to support student success. These include cool zone/ home base and "just walk and don't talk." Each of these strategies (see Table 2.2) will be briefly discussed.

Table 2.2. Rumbling Stage Interventions

- Antiseptic bouncing
- Proximity control
- Signal interference
- Touch control
- Defusing tension through humor

- Support from routine
- Interest boosting
- Cool zone/home base
- "Just walk and don't talk"

Antiseptic bouncing. Antiseptic bouncing involves removing somebody, in a nonpunitive fashion, from the environment in which she is experiencing difficulty. For example, in a school setting, Keisha is asked to take a note to the teacher across the hall. Jerome is asked to go to the art area to clean up supplies.

Similar interventions can be used at work. Andy, who recognizes and understands his rumbling behavior, is delivering a document to a colleague. Because he is "rumbling," he does not go directly from his office down the hall to his colleague. Rather, in order to become better regulated, he stops by the water cooler, goes to the supply room to get some new pens, and then heads to his destination. His way back to his office is equally circuitous. During this time, Andy has had an opportunity to regain a sense of calm so that when he returns to his office, the problem that prompted the rumbling has diminished in magnitude.

Proximity control. Rather than calling attention to somebody's behavior, when using this strategy, the support person moves near the individual who is engaged in "rumbling" behaviors. Often something as simple as standing next to the autistic person is calming and can be easily accomplished without interrupting the event at hand or attracting unnecessary attention. For example, the teacher who circulates through the classroom during a lesson is using proximity control. A reassuring supervisor at the clothing store who moves near an employee when she is signaling "rumbling" by grimacing is also using proximity control.

Signal interference. When the autistic person begins to exhibit a seemingly minor precursor behavior, such as tapping his foot or clearing his throat, the support person gives a non-verbal signal—called signal interference—to let him know that she is aware of the situation. For example, she may place herself in a position from which she can make eye contact with the autistic employee. To help the autistic individual to recognize his or her own distress, a supervisor may use a "secret" signal as a cue.

Touch control. Sometimes a simple touch can stop a rumbling behavior. Gently touching the arm or leg of a student who is tapping his feet loudly may stop the disruptive behavior.

Defusing tension through humor. This technique involves making a joke or humorous remark in a potentially tense moment. When using this approach, care must be taken to ensure that the autistic individual understands the humor and does not perceive himself as the target of a joke. Some personnel are better at using this technique than others. Those who are not "gifted" in this area should not make this their first intervention choice during the Rumbling Stage, as misunderstood humor can lead to escalation to the Rage Stage.

Support from routine. Displaying a chart or visual schedule of expectations and events of the day can provide a sense of security and predictability, which is a central need for most autistics. For example, the student who is signaling frustration by laughing may be directed to her schedule to make her aware that after she completes two more math problems, she gets to work on a topic of special interest with a peer. At work, a gentle reminder that a break will happen in five minutes can be helpful in keeping the employee regulated.

Interest-boosting. Sometimes showing personal interest in an autistic individual and their hobbies can help them become calm. This involves making them aware that you recognize their individual preferences. This also occurs when a task or assignment is shifted to include a special interest. Interest-boosting can often stop rumbling behavior.

Cool zone/home base/break room. Ethan and Amanda Lautenschlager (personal communication, 2004) created the term "cool zone" (which is synonymous with "home base") to describe a place where somebody can go when they feel a need to regain control. For example, a teacher might say, "McKenzie, when it is difficult to finish work, we use the cool zone to help students stay on track. Please take your work to the cool zone." He may then place an icon that says "cool zone" on McKenzie's desk.

The cool zone/home base/break room is typically an environment that does not have a lot of traffic and noise but often contains calming items. For example, somebody who calms by rocking may use a rocking chair in the home base. Those who calm by drawing have access to art supplies.

Going to the cool zone does not mean escaping from work. In fact, work goes with the student, when possible. After the student calms through use of the calming activities in the cool zone, he can then do his work either in the cool zone or in the original environment if he is regulated enough to return.

School resource rooms or counselors' offices can serve as cool zones. Above all, whatever room is chosen must be viewed not as a reward or a disciplinary room but as a place where the student can go to become better regulated. At home, a bedroom or den can be a cool zone or home base. At work, an office or break room can serve this function. Going to the cool zone can prevent the individual from progressing to the Rage Stage.

"Just walk and don't talk." Sometimes (unless the person is a "runner") an effective preventive strategy is to walk with the individual. It is important here for the support person to resist talking because during the Rumbling Stage, the autistic individual is beginning to feel overwhelmed. Any additional input simply adds to the feeling of being overwhelmed and will likely move him to the Rage Stage. In addition, even if the individual is able to process what is being said, anything the support person says is usually the "wrong" thing. The autistic person is not thinking logically and will most likely react emotionally, misinterpreting any statement made by the support person or re-phrasing it in such a way that its original intent is not recognizable. On this walk, the autistic individual can say whatever he wishes without fear of discipline or logical argument. The support person should be calm, show as little reaction as possible, and never be confrontational (Jack Southwick, personal communication, 1999).

When selecting a technique for use during the Rumbling Stage, it is important to know the autistic person, as the wrong strategy can escalate rather than de-escalate a situation. For example, touch control for some students appears to drain off frustration. That is, by merely touching the student's shoulder, the teacher feels immediate relaxation from the student. But another student might be startled by a touch because she (a) did not know the teacher was going to enter her space, (b) misperceived touch as an aggression, or (c) experienced touch as discomforting or painful due to sensory issues. In these cases, touch control would clearly have the opposite effect of the one intended.

Interventions at this stage do not require an extensive outlay of time, but it is important for those who wish to be supportive to watch for and understand the events that precipitate the target behaviors so they can be ready to intervene early or teach strategies to maintain regulation. Please note, however, that autistics cannot be taught these strategies when they are in the Rumbling Stage! Interventions at this stage are merely band-aids. They do not teach ways to recognize or handle stress.

The Rage Stage

If the rumbling behaviors do not stop, the autistic individual is likely to progress to the Rage Stage (see Figure 2.4).

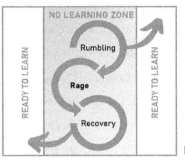

Figure 2.4. Rage Stage

"Behaviors of the Individual"

At this point, the autistic individual is disinhibited and acts impulsively, emotionally, and sometimes explosively. Behaviors may include screaming, biting, hitting, kicking, destroying property, or self-injury. Another type of rage—internal rage—may also manifest. When that is the case, the individual may completely withdraw, unable to verbalize or act in a rational manner (see Table 2.3).

Table 2.3. Typical Rage Behaviors

• Disinhibited	• Destroying property	• Hitting
• Acting impulsively	• Self-injurious	• Kicking
• Emotional	• Screaming	• Experiencing internalizing behavior
• Explosive	• Biting	

Meltdowns are not purposeful, and once the Rage Stage begins, it usually must run its course. Adams (1997) related the following rage incident involving a young boy:

The first meltdown for one young man occurred while in a parking lot. A stranger swore at him and called him a "stupid kid." The boy started to shake a mailbox and began to kick and scream. ... It was noted by the parent that during later attacks, the boy would sometimes say, "I don't want to do this." It appeared that he could not disengage from the emotion, once it had started (p. 72).

Support Person Behaviors

When we find ourselves in situations considered very uncomfortable or dangerous, it is natural to react in a "flight-or-fight" mode. It is not uncommon for a support person to experience this reaction when working with an autistic individual who is in the Rage Stage. It is essential to remain calm—deep breathing can help attain and maintain this state. According to Hubbard (personal communication, 2004), the strategy "less is more" is also helpful for support persons to remember during this stage. In other words, the fewer words the better, the fewer gestures the better, and the fewer movements the better. Strive to make your actions predictable.

Some people manifest rage by raising their voice or yelling. It is important that the support person not respond. Also, the support person should not take the individual's words personally. During this stage, the mouth of the autistic individual is on "automatic pilot," saying words that are unplanned and not included. Those in a support role should disengage emotionally by mentally creating a lesson plan, planning a grocery list, etc.

Generally, support persons should be nonconfrontational and use few words. Individuals at the Rage Stage are not thinking—they are reacting—so words have little meaning. As in the Rumbling Stage, it is important to reevaluate your goal for the autistic person and be flexible. The goal is to move to the Recovery Stage. Table 2.4 lists a series of behaviors that are generally helpful for support persons during the Rage Stage.

Table 2.4. Effective Support Person Behaviors

- Control "flight-or-fight" tendency
- Remember that "less is more"
- Remain calm and quiet
- Do not take behaviors personally
- Disengage emotionally
- Be conscious of your nonverbal cues
- Take deep breaths

Interventions

Since no effective prevention can take place during this stage, emphasis should be placed on the safety of everyone in the environment as well as protection of property. One of the best ways to cope with the rage stage is to get the individual to a cool zone, but only if she can be moved without physical assistance greater than a gentle touch.

Do not discipline or discuss discipline during the Rage Stage—or any other stage. As mentioned, the behavior is not purposeful or planned. Punishing during the Rage Stage would be similar to punishing someone for vomiting.

If the student has a meltdown in front of peers in a school setting, it is often easier to remove the other children. However, to do so, a plan must be in place, and assistance must be obtained to support the autistic child or adolescent or the other students during relocation.

Priority should be placed on helping the individual to regain control and preserving their dignity. Support persons should have developed plans for (a) obtaining assistance; (b) removing the individual from the environment or others from the area, as practical; or (c) providing therapeutic restraint, if necessary. Please note that the latter is almost always unnecessary.

Interventions appropriate for use during the Rage Stage are listed in Table 2.5.

Table 2.5. Rage Stage Interventions

- Protect the student
- Protect the environment
- Protect others
- Don't discipline
- Remove any audience
- Be nonconfrontational
- Plan a "graceful" exit strategy
- Follow a plan
- Obtain assistance
- Prompt to a cool zone, as appropriate
- Use few words
- Prevent a power struggle
- Re-evaluate the student's goals
- Be flexible, since the individual cannot be

Recovery Stage

Although many believe that the crisis cycle ends with the Rage Stage, this is not the case. As shown in Figure 2.5, there is a third stage: the Recovery Stage.

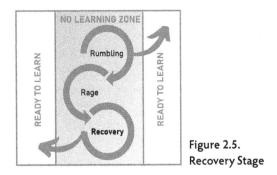

Figure 2.5.
Recovery Stage

"Behaviors" of the Individual

Following the meltdown, the individual with may be contrite and apologize, often without full recall of the meltdown behavior. Or he may become sullen, withdraw, or deny that any inappropriate behavior occurred. Some are so physically exhausted after a meltdown that they just want to sleep (see Table 2.6).

Most often at this stage, the autistic is not ready to learn and should be considered fragile. If not given significant time to calm down after the meltdown, some enter the cycle again and experience a shortened Rumbling Stage that quickly escalates to the Rage Stage.

Table 2.6. Typical Recovery Behavior

- Sleeping
- Denial of rage behaviors
- Withdrawal into fantasy
- Apologizing

Support Person Behaviors

Both the autistic individual and the support person experiencing the meltdown cycle are impacted. Thus, support persons must be aware that they also need time to recover. While it is often not possible for a support person to take time to relax and refocus immediately after the Rage Stage, it is important to schedule time for recovery at some point (see Table 2.7).

Table 2.7. Effective Adult Behavior During the Recovery Stage

- Remain calm and quiet
- Take time for yourself to regroup

If the meltdown occurs at school, the teacher may attempt to relax in the teacher's lounge when her students go to music. At home, the father who was with the child during the meltdown may go out for a drive while the mother stays at home with the child. Perhaps after the child goes to bed, the mother who helped the child through the Rage and Recovery Stage can take a soothing bath. It is important that those who live or work with autistic individuals address their own needs in addition to the needs of others.

Interventions

It is important that the support person works with the autistic individual to help them to once again become a part of the routine or structure, as they are able.

This may be accomplished in several ways, such as:
- Directing the individual to a highly motivating task
- Allowing the individual to work by herself
- Permitting the individual to be in close proximity to a support person
- Encouraging the individual to return to the daily routine with work that is at or below her skill level
- Having the individual use a relaxation strategy (only if it was previously learned and practiced during a teachable moment)

A rule of thumb for interventions during this stage is to use only interventions that are not cognitively draining and that the individual can perform with some degree of mastery. Skills may be considered mastered if they were taught, practiced, and mastered during teachable moments.

Some approaches are almost always counterproductive during the Recovery Stage.
- This is *not* the time to discuss the rage behavior with the individual.
- Do to attempt to teach a new strategy—whether a school or work—even a relaxation strategy.

A list of interventions that can be used during the Recovery Stage is presented in Table 2.8. Remember: meltdowns are not "bad" behavior. They are neurologically based. Thus, these strategies will not be perceived by the autistic person as rewards for the meltdown. Rather, they are intended to help the individual to get ready to learn.

Table 2.8. Recovery Stage Interventions

- Allow the individual to sleep, if necessary
- Support use of relaxation techniques
- Do not refer to the rage behavior
- Support with structure
- Consider the individual to be "fragile"
- Plan instructional interventions to provide alternatives to meltdowns
- Determine appropriate options
- Redirect to successful activity or special interest
- Provide space
- Ensure that interventions are presented at or below the individual's functioning level
- Check to see if the individual is ready to learn/go back to work
- Do not make excessive demands

Ready To Learn

A primary goal when working with autistics who experience the meltdown cycle is to help them learn how to remain regulated. This can happen by:

- Teaching them to understand their environment and themselves
- Structuring the environment for success
- Teaching skills that support academic, social, sensory, and behavioral success

When the Rumbling Stage begins, the support person must recognize the rumbling behaviors and initially intervene to help the individual become ready to learn. However, they must also teach the individual to recognize in themselves their rumbling behaviors and what they can do to move themselves to be ready to learn. This generally takes considerable time and effort. Information about interventions that can prevent meltdowns is presented in Chapter 4.

The ONLY time an individual can learn a skill—whether academic, social, behavioral, or sensory—is when they are not in the Cycle of Meltdowns. Thus, considerable effort must be placed on *preventing* the occurrence of meltdowns so the autistic individual is available to learn.

Summary

To effectively carry out individualized interventions, we must analyze the behaviors that precede challenging situations, as well as those that happen during and after. Instead of random, hit-or-miss efforts, support persons have at their disposal a series of tools whereby they can more closely pinpoint behaviors and their causes. In the following chapter, we will look at a functional behavior assessment (FBA) as a means of accomplishing this critical task.

CHAPTER 3

Overview of Functional Behavior Assessment

"... the core of autism is sometimes missed, due to a tendency to focus too much on the behavior of people with autism (often even details of that behavior) without sufficiently taking into account the context of what is taking place in the mind of people with autism."

(Vermeulen, 2012, p. 353)

In the previous chapter, we discussed the immediate interventions that are helpful in responding to somebody who is in the *middle* of the meltdown cycle: Rumbling, Rage, and Recovery. However, it is also important to be knowledgeable about strategies that minimize or prevent the occurrence of meltdowns in the first place.

To prevent the cycle of meltdowns, it is important to understand the function(s) or purpose(s) of the behavior(s) exhibited during Rumbling, Rage, and Recovery. This process is known as functional behavior assessment (FBA). FBA is designed to answer the question, "Why does Johnny _____?" As such, it is a first step in developing effective interventions. Indeed, without determining the reasons, causes, or conditions under which a behavior occurs, interventions are not likely to be effective.

The following six steps comprise a functional behavior assessment and the resulting behavior intervention plan (FBA/BIP):

1. Identify and describe behavior.
2. Describe setting demands and antecedents.
3. Collect baseline data and/or work samples.
4. Complete functional analysis measures and develop a hypothesis.
5. Develop and implement a behavioral intervention plan.
6. Collect data and follow up to analyze the effectiveness of the plan (Aspy, Grossman, Myles, & Henry, 2016).

While an in-depth discussion of how to conduct an FBA is beyond the scope of this book, in the following we provide an overview of how to adapt the FBA/BIP process to address the underlying needs of autistic individuals—a critical and helpful process.

The Iceberg Metaphor

Traditional FBAs examine behavior as it relates to what occurs *before* (antecedents) and what occurs *after* (consequences) the behavior of interest. In addition, traditional FBAs look at a limited number of functions: escape, avoidance, access to tangible or social reinforcement, and sensory stimulation. However, these functions are superficial because they do not address how the individual's autism impacts the behavior under scrutiny.

Schopler (1994) used an iceberg as a metaphor to illustrate the notion that visible behaviors (the portion of the iceberg above the surface of the water) are manifestations of underlying or "hidden" characteristics of autism (the portion of the iceberg beneath the surface of the water). According to Schopler, effective behavior interventions must address underlying needs and not simply visible or "surface" behaviors (see Figure 3.1).

The Underlying Characteristics of Autism

Targeting underlying needs will lead to interventions that are more proactive and fundamental than those in a traditional FBA. By contrast, interventions that solely address surface behavior without consideration of the underlying autism are potentially

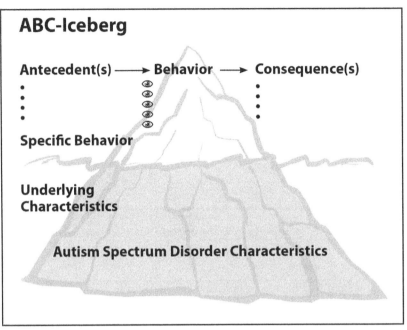

Figure 3.1. Underlying Characteristics of Autism

From Aspy, R., & Grossman, B. G. (2022). The Ziggurat Model: A Framework for Designing Comprehensive Strategies and Supports for Autistic Individuals Release 2.1. Dallas, TX: The Ziggurat Group. Used with permission.

less effective and less likely to result in sustained behavior change. As illustrated by the Ziggurat Model (Aspy & Grossman, 2022), "Consideration of patterns of behavior in addition to underlying characteristics will lead to a better understanding of specific behavioral concerns and their unseen causes" (p. 47).

The best way to understand a behavior is to look at the individual's autism characteristics and how they are reflected in the behavior. The Underlying Characteristics Checklist (UCC; Aspy & Grossman, 2022) is designed to do just that. Alternatively, when working with a staff that is well trained and experienced in the area of autism, the underlying characteristics may be identified from observations. Figure 3.2 shows the first page of the UCC:

UCC-HF
UNDERLYING CHARACTERISTICS CHECKLIST
HIGH FUNCTIONING

The Ziggurat Group

RUTH ASPY, PH.D., AND BARRY G. GROSSMAN, PH.D.

NAME: _____   DATE: _____   COMPLETED BY: _____

FOLLOW-UP DATE: _____   COMPLETED BY: _____

INSTRUCTIONS FOR COMPLETING INITIAL ASSESSMENT:
The UCC may be completed by an individual; however, the perspective of others who know and/or work with the person of focus is beneficial. Working as a team is optimal. Additionally, the team may include the individual who is the focus of the UCC as developmentally appropriate.

Please place a check beside ALL items that currently apply to the individual. Use the **Notes** column to describe the behavior and characteristics in more detail, provide specific examples, or indicate frequency, settings, etc.

At the end of each section, in the **Individual Strengths and Skills** box, list the individual's strengths and skills related to each area.

PROJECTED FOLLOW-UP DATE: _____

AREA	ITEM	✓	NOTES	FOLLOW-UP
SOCIAL	1. Has difficulty recognizing the feelings and thoughts of others (mindblindness)	✓	• Does not recognize when classmates tease or "set her up" • After being corrected at home, she repetitively asks her parents if they are still angry • In role plays, she can accurately identify the feelings of others 4 out of 10 times	
	2. Uses poor eye contact			
	3. Has difficulty maintaining personal space, physically intrudes on others	✓	• Sniffs peers' hair	

INSTRUCTIONS FOR FOLLOW-UP ASSESSMENT:
Review checked and unchecked items. Use the **Notes** column to add further descriptors or to indicate changes. If the item no longer applies, strike through the check and explain changes in the **Follow-Up** column, as illustrated below.

AREA	ITEM	✓	NOTES	FOLLOW-UP
SOCIAL	1. Has difficulty recognizing the feelings and thoughts of others (mindblindness)	✓	• Does not recognize when classmates tease or "set her up" • After being corrected at home, she repetitively asks her parents if they are still angry • In role plays, she can accurately identify the feelings of others 4 out of 10 times	• Accurately reported that she was being teased last week • In role plays, she can now accurately identify others' feelings 6 out of 10 times
	2. Uses poor eye contact			
	3. Has difficulty maintaining personal space, physically intrudes on others	✗	• Sniffs peers' hair	• No longer sniffs others. Follows rules for respecting personal space of others

Figure 3.2. First Page of the UCC-High Functioning

From Aspy, R., & Grossman, B.G. (2022). Underlying characteristics checklist: Self-Report Adolescent. Dallas TX: The Ziggurat Group. Used with permission.

High-Functioning. Other versions of the instrument include UCC: Self-Report Adolescent (Aspy & Grossman, 2022), UCC: Classic (Aspy & Grossman, 2022), UCC: Early Intervention (Aspy & Grossman, 2022), UCC: Self-Report Adult (Aspy & Grossman, 2022).

Miguel: Case Illustration

Miguel is a fourth-grade student who is being serviced in special education under the category of autism. Academically he is at or above grade level in all areas. Miguel is fascinated by the Revolutionary War and often reads college-level books about that period of U.S. history. Miguel enters the Rumbling Stage each time he is given an assignment from a new unit in the math book. His rumbling behaviors include talking to himself, rocking in his chair, and erasing his paper so hard that a hole starts to appear. He escalates to the Rage Stage by wadding up his paper, throwing it on the floor, and crying. He is reprimanded for his behavior and sent to the office if he does not calm immediately. In addition, his daily report to his parents documents loss of points for negative behavior.

Figure 3.3 shows an FBA-Iceberg (Aspy & Grossman, 2022) for Miguel completed through the use of a UCC.

Once the UCC is completed, interventions are matched to each characteristic that is related to the behavior with a focus on comprehensive interventions. This occurs when each behavior is viewed from the lens of autism: Sensory Differences and Biological Needs, Reinforcement, Structure and Visual/Tactile Supports, Obstacle Removal, and Skills to Teach (see Table 3.1). The Ziggurat Model allows this to happen.

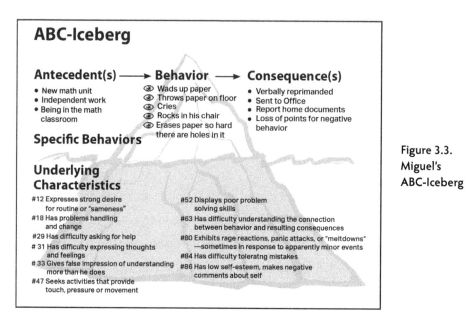

ABC-Iceberg

Antecedent(s) ⟶ **Behavior** ⟶ **Consequence(s)**

- New math unit
- Independent work
- Being in the math classroom

- ⊘ Wads up paper
- ⊘ Throws paper on floor
- ⊘ Cries
- ⊘ Rocks in his chair
- ⊘ Erases paper so hard there are holes in it

- Verbally reprimanded
- Sent to Office
- Report home documents
- Loss of points for negative behavior

Specific Behaviors

Underlying Characteristics

#12 Expresses strong desire for routine or "sameness"
#18 Has problems handling and change
#29 Has difficulty asking for help
31 Has difficulty expressing thoughts and feelings
33 Gives false impression of understanding more than he does
#47 Seeks activities that provide touch, pressure or movement

#52 Displays poor problem solving skills
#63 Has difficulty understanding the connection between behavior and resulting consequences
#80 Exhibits rage reactions, panic attacks, or "meltdowns" —sometimes in response to apparently minor events
#84 Has difficulty tolerating mistakes
#86 Has low self-esteem, makes negative comments about self

Figure 3.3. Miguel's ABC-Iceberg

From Aspy, R., & Grossman, B.G. (2022). The Ziggurat Model: A Framework for Designing Comprehensive Strategies and Supports for Autistic Individuals Release 2.1. Dallas, TX: The Ziggurat Group.

Table 3.1. Levels of the Ziggurat Model

Level	Description
Skills to Teach	Interventions that focus on teaching critical skills (often those that neuromajority peers learn without direct instruction)
Task Demands and Positive Environment	Interventions that involve changing the demands of a setting or task so that the individual with autism is able to participate successfully
Structure and Visual/Tactile Supports	Interventions related to routines and predictability as well as presentation of important information in a visual manner *Note:* If the autistic has a vision impairment, the supports would be tactile instead of visual.
Respectful Reinforcement	Preferred items or activities to increase the likelihood of positive behaviors
Sensory and Biological	Interventions that address proprioceptive, vestibular, auditory, visual, olfactory, gustatory, interoception, and tactile, as well as supports for sleep, nutrition, and medical conditions, including seizures and catatonia

Each of Miguel's underlying characteristics—salient to his target behavior—is then matched to interventions across the five levels of the Ziggurat Model (see Table 3.2).

Table 3.2. Miguel's UCC Items Matched to Interventions and Levels

Items from Miguel's UCC	Interventions* Based on Underlying Characteristics	Ziggurat Levels
• Expresses strong need for routine or "sameness" • Has problems handling transition and change • Gives false impression of understanding more than he does • Displays poor problem-solving skills • Exhibits rage reactions or "meltdowns" • Has difficulty tolerating mistakes	Use a visual calendar that shows when new units in math will begin	Structure and Visual/Tactile Support
• Expresses strong need for routine or "sameness" • Has problems handling transition and change • Gives false impression of understanding more than he does • Displays poor problem-solving skills • Exhibits rage reactions or "meltdowns" • Has difficulty tolerating mistakes	Prime prior to new math units	Task Demands and Positive Environment
• Expresses strong need for routine or "sameness" • Has problems handling transition and change • Has difficulty expressing thoughts and feelings • Gives false impression of understanding more than he does • Displays poor problem-solving skills • Has difficulty understanding the connection between behavior and resulting consequences • Exhibits rage reactions or "meltdowns" • Has difficulty tolerating mistakes	Use a Stress Thermometer that indicates levels of stress and interventions that support each level	Structure and Visual/Tactile Support

* See Chapter 4 for more details about interventions.

Table 3.2 continued

• Has problems handling transition and change • Has difficulty expressing thoughts and feelings • Has difficulty understanding the connection between behavior and resulting consequences • Exhibits rage reactions or "meltdowns" • Has difficulty tolerating mistakes	Role-play using interventions on the Stress Thermometer to teach emotions and identify behaviors in self and interventions	Skills to Teach
• Expresses strong need for routine or "sameness" • Has problems handling transition and change • Has difficulty asking for help • Has difficulty expressing thoughts and feelings • Displays poor problem-solving skills • Has difficulty understanding the connection between behavior and resulting consequences • Exhibits rage reactions or "meltdowns"	Check in to ask Miguel to point to his stress level on the Stress Thermometer	Task Demands and Positive Environment
• Expresses strong need for routine or "sameness" • Has difficulty expressing thoughts and feelings • Has difficulty understanding the connection between behavior and resulting consequences • Exhibits rage reactions or "meltdowns" • Has difficulty tolerating mistakes	Reinforce Miguel for pointing to stress level and using strategies	Respectful Reinforcement
• Expresses strong need for routine or "sameness" • Has difficulty expressing thoughts and feelings • Has difficulty understanding the connection between behavior and resulting consequences • Exhibits rage reactions or "meltdowns" • Has difficulty tolerating mistakes	Teach Miguel about his feelings and emotions using the Interoception Curriculum (Mahler, 2019)	Skills to Teach

Table 3.2 continued

• Has problems handling transition and change • Has difficulty expressing thoughts and feelings • Displays poor problem-solving skills • Has difficulty understanding the connection between behavior and resulting consequences • Exhibits rage reactions or "meltdowns" • Has difficulty tolerating mistakes • Has low self-esteem, makes negative comments about self	Use cartooning to illustrate the sequence of events as well as an alternative sequence of events when he uses calming strategies	Structure and Visual/Tactile Support
• Has problems handling transition and change • Displays poor problem-solving skills • Has difficulty understanding the connection between behavior and resulting consequences • Exhibits rage reactions or "meltdowns" • Has difficulty tolerating mistakes	Teach Miguel to use the Problem-Solving Rubric (Mataya & Owens, 2013)	Skills to Teach
• Has difficulty asking for help • Has difficulty tolerating mistakes • Exhibits rage reactions or "meltdowns" • Has low self-esteem, makes negative comments about self • Displays poor problem-solving skills • Gives false impression of understanding more than he does	Use nonverbal prompts to support Miguel in using the strategies	Structure and Visual/Tactile Support
• Gives false impression of understanding more than he does • Exhibits rage reactions or "meltdowns" • Has difficulty tolerating mistakes • Has low self-esteem; makes negative comments about self	Reinforce use of math skills	Respectful Reinforcement
• Gives false impression of understanding more than he does • Displays poor problem-solving skills • Has difficulty understanding the connection between behavior and resulting consequences • Exhibits rage reactions or "meltdowns" • Has difficulty tolerating mistakes	Remove any competitive elements from math, such as timed assignments and sharing of grades	Task Demands and Positive Environment

Table 3.2 continued

• Displays poor problem-solving skills • Exhibits rage reactions or "meltdowns" • Has difficulty tolerating mistakes • Has low self-esteem, makes negative comments about self	Review past "new units" with Miguel to illustrate that he can do math and that "new units" become mastered skills	Skills to Teach
• Seeks activities that provide touch, pressure, or movement • Exhibits rage reactions or "meltdowns"	Use TheraBands™ to provide Miguel with touch and pressure or allow Miguel to sit on a therapy ball, as recommended by the occupational therapist (OT)	Sensory and Biological
• Seeks activities that provide touch, pressure, or movement • Exhibits rage reactions or "meltdowns"	Ensure that Miguel's sensory interventions recommended by the OT are followed in the math room	Sensory and Biological
• Has difficulty understanding the connection between behavior and resulting consequences • Exhibits rage reactions or "meltdowns" • Has low self-esteem; makes negative comments about self	After he has completed a math assignment, permit Miguel to share a Revolutionary War fact with the class	Respectful Reinforcement

Each of the levels is essential and contributes to the effectiveness of the others. Thus, if an individual's needs on *all* levels are not addressed, the intervention will not be as effective, and skills will not develop.

The following table provides a comparison of Miguel's interventions using a traditional FBA which focuses on antecedents, behaviors, and consequences (A-B-C) and the more comprehensive FBA-Iceberg.

Which of the two types of interventions is more likely to meet Miguel's needs and lead to ongoing behavior change and skill development? The FBA-Iceberg! Miguel's underlying characteristics listed on the FBA-Iceberg were selected because of the relationship between the specific UCC items and his behavior of concern. They directly address

Table 3.3. Interventions Based on Antecedents-Behaviors-Consequences vs. Those Based on Underlying Characteristics

Interventions Based on A-B-C	Interventions* Based on Underlying Characteristics
Provide "double points" for Miguel when he begins a new math unit	Use a visual calendar that shows when new units in math will begin
Send home a report of Miguel's behavior, both positive and negative	Prime prior to new math units
Give Miguel fewer math problems	Use a Stress Thermometer that indicates levels of stress and interventions that support each level
Have Miguel bring new units in the resource room	Role-play using interventions on the Stress Thermometer to teach emotions and identify behaviors in self and interventions
	Check in to ask Miguel to point to his stress level on the Stress Thermometer
	Reinforce Miguel for pointing to stress level and using strategies
	Teach Miguel about his feelings and emotions using the Interoception Curriculum (Mahler, 2019)
	Use cartooning to illustrate the sequence of events as well as an alternative sequence of events when he uses calming strategies
	Teach Miguel to use the Problem-Solving Rubric (Mataya & Owens, 2013)
	Use nonverbal prompts to support Miguel in using the strategies
	Reinforce use of math skills
	Remove any competitive elements from math, such as timed assignments and sharing of grades
	Review past "new units" with Miguel to illustrate that he can do math and that "new units" become mastered skills
	Use TheraBands™ to provide Miguel with touch and pressure or allow Miguel to sit on a therapy ball, as recommended by the occupational therapist (OT)
	Ensure that Miguel's sensory interventions recommended by the OT are followed in the math room
	After he has completed a math assignment, permit Miguel to share a Revolutionary War fact with the class

* See Chapter 4 for more details about interventions.

Miguel's autism and go beyond one situation in which he is experiencing difficulty. The interventions on the FBA-Iceberg that Miguel uses here can be helpful for him in other academic and nonacademic settings.

Summary

Most autistic individuals demonstrate differences in multiple areas: social, interests, communication, sensory, cognitive, motor, and emotional. These differences, which are very real but sometimes difficult for others to see and understand, often make what seem to be routine events especially challenging.

The traditional FBA, which focuses on antecedents, behaviors, and consequences (A-B-C), results in interventions directly linked to those three areas. The Ziggurat FBA-Iceberg presented in this chapter goes one step further by considering the relationship between an individual's autism and the target behavior. As such, interventions are directly targeted to the underlying characteristics, not strictly to the surface behaviors, and therefore result in more meaningful change across environments.

Some individuals have developed coping and calming strategies that allow them to spend most of their time in a regulated state; however, because of the ongoing challenges that autism characteristics present, many spend significant portions of their lives in the Rumbling Stage. Strategies that help a person to transition from the Rumbling Stage to the regulated Ready to Learn state may be needed daily in order to stay out of crisis—able to learn and participate within school, work, or community environments. Such strategies are presented in the following chapter.

CHAPTER 4

Strategies
That Promote
Regulation

A utistics do not want to engage in meltdowns. But for most, the meltdown cycle is the only way they have available to them to express stress, anxiety, problems with coping, or a host of other emotions and situations to which they see no immediate solution. This chapter discusses interventions that have been found to be effective for minimizing or eliminating meltdowns.

The best intervention for meltdowns is to teach skills to prevent their occurrence. However, as mentioned in Chapter 2, prevention strategies are effective only when the individual is not embroiled in the cycle of meltdowns. "Ready to Learn" moments are exclusive to times when the individual is calm, focused, and relaxed (see Figure 2.1).

In order to break the meltdown cycle, it is important to support the development and use of skills and social understanding—the absence of which can lead to meltdowns. Instruction, interpretation, coaching, and obstacle removal are addressed for the autistic individual who experiences meltdowns and the staff who support them.

Note. Many of the interventions described in this chapter fit into more than one of the four categories defined below. For example, social narratives can serve as both an instructional and an interpretive tool.

Instruction

Instruction refers to the process of teaching and engagement of learners—children, adolescents, and adults alike. To ensure appropriate and effective instruction of self-regulation skills, it is necessary to identify which skills are present and where skills break down in the face of daily demands. This is true for the autistic person *and* the support person.

Instruction for the Autistic Individual

Autistic individuals demonstrate many challenges and differences that require instruction to ensure they acquire skills that facilitate self-regulation—the major focus of this chapter. Most often, they do not automatically acquire many skills that are otherwise taken for granted without a planned instructional sequence. An absence of these skills may lead to becoming overwhelmed and entering the Cycle of Meltdowns.

A common error in working with autistic individuals is to become blinded by their strengths.

- The fact that somebody can identify expressions of emotions in pictures does not mean that he can identify the same emotions in a real-life interaction.
- Even if someone can list the four steps to problem solving, that does not mean that she can independently utilize the steps when faced with a challenge.
- An individual who can list and describe the battles of the Revolutionary War may not be able to transition to a new math unit without becoming overwhelmed by the change.

The following interventions will be discussed:

    a. scope and sequence   e. acting lessons

    b. direct instruction   f. self-esteem building

    c. social narratives   g. multimedia lessons

    d. hidden curriculum

Scope and Sequence

It is important to observe and carefully consider how somebody functions during actual tasks in real-life environments in order to accurately figure out her skill level. A range of task demands must be analyzed—noise level, age of others in environment, number of people in environment, availability of visual supports, length of task, time of day, temperature, and an infinite list of other factors.

A scope-and-sequence chart, such as the one by Baker (2023) presented in Table 4.1, is helpful for identifying skill gaps or deficits. While the entire scope and sequence includes ninety-two skills that teach communication and emotion management skills to autistic children and adolescents and related exceptionalities, items presented here relate directly to regulation. Supported by many years of use in a clinical setting, Baker's scope and sequence is accompanied by an easy-to-use assessment measure that can be used by parents and educators. The assessment is unique in that it assesses not only whether the individual has a given skill, but also how often to use it.

Table 4.1. Baker's Scope and Sequence of Emotion Regulation Issues

1. Recognizing Emotions

2. Discriminating the Size of Emotions

3. Understanding the Connection between Events, Thoughts, and Emotions

4. Understanding Our Alarm System: Hulk versus Dr. Banner

5. Keeping Calm

6. Problem-Solving

7. Talking versus Acting Out Feelings

8. Understanding Your Anger: Using the Daily Anger Record

9. Using a Growth Mindset to Manage Frustration

10. Trying When Work Is Hard

11. Dealing with Making a Mistake

12. Accepting No and Waiting for What You Want

13. Stopping a Fun Activity

14. Dealing with Anxiety and Fear: Understanding the Alarm Reaction

15. Manage Fears by Creating a Fear Ladder

16. Manage Fears by Thinking Like a Scientist

17. Manage Fears through Physical Ways

18. Dealing with Unpleasant Obsessive Thoughts and Compulsive Behaviors

19. Dealing with Social Fears

20. Dealing with Brief Periods of Depression

From Social Skills Training for Children and Adolescents with Autism and Other Social-Communication Differences, 20th Anniversary Edition *by Jed Baker. Copyright 2023 by Future Horizons. Used with permission.*

Because autistic individuals often have an uneven profile of social, behavioral, and communication skills, it is important to understand the sequence in which these skills develop. Without an understanding of scope and sequence, it is possible to overlook the fact that a person may be missing an important prerequisite skill that might make a more advanced skill become rote instead of a usable asset. For example, if a child does not understand that tone of voice beyond the actual words used communicates a message, then teaching the more advanced skill of using a respectful tone of voice to adults has little or no meaning. If the individual learns by rote to use that tone of voice, she will probably not be able to generalize it. The following materials, developed for autistic individuals, also offer scope-and-sequence charts.

Navigating the Social World: A Curriculum for Individuals With Asperger's Syndrome, High Functioning Autism, and Related Disabilities by McAfee (2013) contains a list of twenty social/ emotional skills that address (a) recognizing and coping with one's emotions, (b) communication and social skills, (c) abstract thinking skills, and (d) behavior issues. This scope and sequence (and accompanying lessons) seems particularly appropriate for autistic girls and related challenges. That is not surprising, as this resource was developed by a mother, who is a pediatrician, for her daughter.

Building Social Relationships 2 by Bellini (2016). This book provides a comprehensive five-step model for social and relationship development that includes assessing social functioning, distinguishing between skill acquisition and performance deficits, selecting intervention strategies, implementing intervention, and evaluating and monitoring progress.

Direct Instruction

Unlike how most of their neuromajority peers seem to do so, most autistics do not automatically develop the social and behavioral skills necessary to be successful in school, home, and the community. As a result, support persons must provide direct instruction on these skills using a consistent lesson plan format incorporating traditional as well as nontraditional curricula.

Lesson Plan:

A lesson plan is an instructional sequence that facilitates skill acquisition, including

a. rationale

b. presentation

c. modeling

d. verification

e. evaluation

f. generalization

Each lesson should incorporate these six elements, as reviewed below.

Rationale. In order to learn, many autistics need to understand how or why concepts required for mastery are relevant. Thus, support persons must relate (a) why the information is useful, (b) how it can be used, and (c) where it fits with the knowledge the individual already possesses. The rationale should include a visual task analysis that illustrates all the components of the lesson, including the amount of time to be spent on the lesson and which activities to complete.

One helpful guideline in teaching new skills is: **Never tell what to do without telling why.** Providing the reason for using a skill often adds information about what others in the environment may think or feel in response to specific behaviors. This rationale is important for individuals for whom some degree of mind-blindness (Vermeulen, 2012) may be present. It also increases the likelihood that the skill will generalize.

Presentation. Once the rationale has been introduced, the support person works with the individual to identify goals for the content. Then, using a direct instructional format, including both visual and auditory stimuli, the content is taught. Information is broken down into small increments and then presented. This type of instruction is active, with the support person sharing information, asking questions, and providing corrective feedback. In addition, it is essential to incorporate discussion and/or multiple illustrations of *context* and *prediction*, which will strengthen the ability of the autistic person to understand and use the skill being taught. In other words, direct instruction does *not* mean presenting a worksheet with a model and telling the individual to follow the directions.

Modeling. During the modeling phase, the support person first obtains the individual's attention and shows her what the skill or strategy looks like when used. For example, the support person may demonstrate (a) how to make a 911 telephone call calmly, (b) how to enter a group discussion at work, or (c) how to breathe deeply and think about a special interest as a way to become self-regulated when overwhelmed. The emphasis should be placed on what to do instead of what not to do. This is particularly important as many autistics know what *not* to do but have little understanding of what is required of them.

Every direction is explicitly spelled out, preferably using a visual support. The support person cannot infer that the individual understands a concept or format just because it has been presented before. Anything that is merely implied will likely not be understood. Models should be presented frequently.

Verification. Verification means making certain that the individual is "with you" during instruction and understands the information presented. Throughout the lesson, the support person closely monitors the individual's emotional state. Because autistics may have a flat, even seemingly negative affect, it may be difficult to tell, for example, when they are stressed as a result of not understanding specific content. The support person must work with the individual to understand how he or she communicates emotional distress and meet his needs as necessary through additional instruction, modeling, or individual work sessions. Failure to engage the individual in this very important step can result in him "tuning out" or, worse yet, having a meltdown.

The individual must be actively engaged throughout the instructional process. For example, he may be provided physical cues to attend to relevant stimuli and be asked questions frequently. Physical cues could take the form of the support person using proximity control or a prearranged signal, such as clearing the throat or placing a hand on the individual's shoulder (see Chapter 2).

For the autistic person who requires a long processing time or has difficulty with prediction, the support person might present questions far in advance. In school, a support person might share a "secret signal" that alerts the student that a question is forthcoming. For example, a teacher might tell the student that she will only be asked a question when the teacher stands next to her. When using this strategy, the teacher initially asks the student questions to which the student already knows the answers.

As the student becomes comfortable with the strategy and thus more confident, the teacher can introduce questions that are more difficult. (No one else in the class needs to know that the student and teacher have this agreement.)

Evaluation. Following instruction, both the support person and the autistic individual must evaluate skill acquisition. They should employ a variety of methods, such as role-play and video modeling, to assess understanding and use of the skill, including self-evaluating skill use and setting goals for generalization and maintenance.

Generalization. Programming for generalization must be a part of every instructional sequence by arranging opportunities for autistics to use newly acquired skills throughout the day and in a variety of settings. Support persons should also observe the individual in less structured settings, such as in a restaurant, store, or movie theater, to determine whether the skill has truly been generalized. Finally, assistance from family members is invaluable for ensuring generalization. Specifically, they can set up and/or observe home- and community-based events in which the individual would be expected to use the skills.

Curricula

Several traditional curricula (that is, curricula designed for autistic students for use by educational professionals, support persons, and clinicians) may be used to provide direct instruction.

*Talk With Me: A Step-by-Step Conversation Framework for Teaching Conversation Balance and Fluency**
by Mataya, Aspy, and Hollis (2017) breaks down the

elements of a conversation that must be mastered be proficient at carrying out a conversation. The framework was developed and refined across many years based on a review of the relevant research along with close observation of how people talk to each other— what conversations really sound like. The Conversation Framework provides a simple and easy-to-implement process that is specific enough to equip an autistic individual with the tools necessary to acquire conversation skills and simple enough to be used at any age.

Navigating the Social World: A Curriculum for Individuals With Asperger's Syndrome, High Functioning Autism, and Related Disorders by McAfee (2013) is a user-friendly program addressing social and emotional challenges. This curriculum was developed specifically for autistic girls.

Peer Play and the Autism Spectrum: The Art of Guiding Children's Socialization and Imagination the award-winning book by Wolfberg (2003) teaches adults how to set up play groups with typical peers and autistic children. Everything needed to set up and carry out play groups is included.

Curricula for peers

Helping autistic individuals develop friendships and participate in support networks is integral to their success and often to their overall happiness. Because the desire for social interactions is typically high, involving peers is usually a strong motivator. In addition, doing so provides an excellent venue to practice social skills—for both the autistic and the neuromajority peer.

As such, it is helpful if neuromajority peers understand some of the autistic individual's underlying characteristics, strengths, and needs, such as allowing extra time to answer a question, saying their name first to get the individual's attention, and being equipped with support strategies. Peer support can be designed to be a "two-way street." The autistic individual contributes strengths and skills while his partners contribute their strengths and skills. When peer supports are provided so that the individual can interact successfully, positive relationships with peers become more likely.

The Organization for Autism Research developed the **Kit for Kids,** which is designed to teach elementary and middle school students about their autistic pers. Available at no cost (https://researchautism.org/educators/kit-for-kids/#whats-up-with-nick-booklets), the kit is centered around an illustrated booklet entitled *What's up with Nick.* The booklet, told through the eyes of a neuromajority peer, teaches children and youth through grade eight that autistic students may think differently and may need some supports, but they are worthy individuals in their own right and should be treated with respect. The comprehensive kit contains lesson plans, a poster, online resources, and other supplemental materials.

Social Narratives

Social narratives are brief, written paragraphs that provide support and instruction for autistic children and adolescents by describing social cues and appropriate responses to social behavior and teaching new social skills. Written by educators or parents at the child's instructional level and often using pictures or photographs to supplement the content, social narratives can promote self-awareness, self-calming, and self-management. Minimal guidelines exist for creating social narratives other than to ensure that the content matches the student's needs and takes the student's perspective into account (Myles, Trautman, & Schelvan, 2013).

Social narratives may either illuminate or celebrate a skill that was demonstrated well or describe a situation that is challenging. At least half of the narratives used with any given individual should be positive, celebratory narratives. This helps to reinforce new skills and prevent students from ignoring or avoiding narratives simply because they tend to focus on previous struggles.

Table 4.2 provides a set of guidelines that may be used to structure a social narrative.

Table 4.2. Guidelines for Constructing Social Narratives

1. Identify a challenging situation or a skill in which the individual has been successful. The first time that social narratives are used, it is important to highlight individual successes. A behavior addressed in a social narrative should result in (a) increased positive social interactions, (b) a safer environment, and/or (c) additional social learning opportunities. The behavior should be task-analyzed and based on the individual's current skills.

2. Define target behavior or knowledge. The individuals who plan and implement social narratives must clearly define the behavior or situation in a way that the individual can understand.

3. Write the social narrative. The narrative should be written in accordance with the individual's comprehension skills, with vocabulary and print size individualized. The stories should be written in the

first or third person and either in the present (to describe a situation as it occurs) or the future tense (to anticipate an upcoming event).

4. Display the narrative in a way that is commensurate with the individual's level of understanding. Depending on the individual's processing ability, more than one sentence per page may result in an overload of information, preventing him from comprehending. For some, up to three sentences per page is acceptable. Each sentence allows the individual to focus on and process a specific concept. Pictorial representations can enhance understanding of appropriate behavior, especially for those with limited reading skills. Sometimes the individual for whom the story is written provides the illustrations. Decisions about whether to use drawings, pictures, or icons should be made on an individual basis.

5. Read the social narrative. The teacher or person should read the social narrative as a consistent part of the daily schedule. Further, the individual who reads independently may read the social narrative to others so that all have a similar perspective of the targeted situation and corresponding appropriate behaviors.

6. Review findings. If desired changes fail to occur after the social narrative has been implemented for two weeks, the narrative and its implementation procedures should be reviewed.

7. Program for maintenance and generalization. After a behavior change has been established consistently, use of the social narrative may be faded. Fading may be accomplished by extending the time between readings or by placing additional responsibility on the autistic individual for reading her own social narratives.

There are many types of social narratives, including: (a) Social Stories™ (Gray, 2016) descriptive stories, (b) scripts, (c) the Power Card Strategy (Gagnon & Myles (2016), and (d) conversation starters, as described below.

Social Stories™

Undoubtably the most recognized among social narratives is Carol Gray's Social Stories™. Introduced in 1993 by Gray and Garand, the intervention has evolved over time from audio recordings to written stories; from text only to including photos, icons, and drawings; and from being individualized stories to pre-created stories, as illustrated in the book, *The New Social Story Book: The Revised and Expanded 15th Anniversary Edition*, which offers over 150 Social Stories™ (Gray, 2016). A Social Story™ includes a title, introduction, body, and conclusion. It uses positive language that addresses where, when, who, what, how and why. Coaching sentences may also be included. More information about Social Stories™ can be found at https://carolgraysocialstories.com.

Descriptive Stories

A descriptive story explains a situation, usually from the autistic individual's point of view. Descriptive stories are generally short and are written at a level that the learner can easily understand. They often include pictures that help explain the story.

One of the best ways to write a descriptive story is to use flexible words, such as "usually," "sometimes," "often," "may," and "most of the time." Autistics are often very literal, so if a flexible word is not used, they may experience difficulty interpreting the story if the details of a situation do not completely match the narrative.

Each descriptive story is different depending on what is important for the individual to be successful. Descriptive stories may:

- Tell what the individual will see, smell, hear, or feel
- Describe the sequence of activities
- Tell what other people might be doing

- Describe what the individual should do in the given situation
- Encourage the individual to try to participate
- Remind the individual of reinforcers that will be available at the end of the activity
- Describe what others might think or feel
- Describe what the individual might think or feel
- Describe supports or help that the individual can receive in the activity

A descriptive story about riding on the bus might begin with the phrase, "I rode on the bus to the zoo." The entire descriptive story follows.

I Rode on the Bus to the Zoo

I rode on the bus to the zoo. During most of the ride, I wore my headphones and listened to Beyonce. I felt happy when I got to the zoo. Ms. Tutu was proud of me, and she said, "You did such a good job on the bus. Your headphones really helped you have a good bus ride." I am proud of myself.

The following is a descriptive story for an adolescent who became upset when the schedule changed.

When My Schedule Changes

Sometimes I get angry when schedules change. Teachers usually tell me before things change. Sometimes teachers cannot tell me before things change. I will try to ask a teacher what to do if I am confused about the new schedule. It will be easier for her to understand what I need if I am not crying or yelling. Schedules can be changed, and it is okay to follow a new schedule. When the schedule is changed, my teacher will be there to help me.

Social Scripts

Social scripts provide ready-to-use language for specific events. They may be structured as conversation starters, scripted responses, or cues to change topics (cf. Leaf et al., 2020). For instance, an autistic individual may practice a script that includes key questions that can help him to begin a conversation. For the autistic person who has trouble spontaneously generating language, social scripts are effective because they help with language recall.

When designing social scripts, care should be taken to include "context-friendly language." That is, common jargon should be incorporated as well as the informal language style used by peers.

The following is a script for a school-aged individual.

Asking Questions in Class

If you want to ask questions in class, here are some words that you can use with your teacher:

1. May I ask a question?

2. I have a question.

3. Would you please say that again?

The next script was created for a young adult with who did not know what to say to a professor regarding the supports he needed at the university.

Requesting Supports at the University Level

Excuse me, my name is Frank Masters, and I am really enjoying your class. I have a disability and need some accommodations. I will be recording your lectures on my phone so that I can listen to them a couple of times to make sure that I can learn what you are teaching. Also, I need more time to take tests, so the Office of Exceptionalities has arranged for me to take your tests in the study lab. Mr. Johnson will email you to make these arrangements. I hope that this is okay. Thank you. And again, I am really enjoying your class.

The Power Card Strategy

The Power Card Strategy is a visually based technique that uses a person's special interest to facilitate understanding of social situations, routines, and the meaning of language (Gagnon & Myles, 2016; Prince et al., 2023). The intervention contains two components: a script and a Power Card. A support person writes a brief script at the individual's comprehension level detailing the problem situation or target behavior. The script includes a description of the behavior and a statement of how the individual's special interest/hero has addressed the same social challenge. The individual is encouraged to use the same strategy to address a specific situation.

The second component of the strategy, The Power Card, which is the size of a business card or trading card, contains a picture of the special interest and a summary of the solution. Portable to promote generalization, the Power Card may be carried or Velcroed® inside a book, notebook, or locker or kept in a wallet or billfold. Figure 4.1 provides a sample script and Power Card used to support a high school student.

Hidden Curriculum

Everyone knows that Mrs. Kristmann allows students to whisper in class as long as they get their work done, whereas Mrs. Rafik does not tolerate even the faintest level of noise in her class. Everyone knows that Howard Johnson, the floor supervisor, is a stickler for clocking in and out, so arrival at work and clocking in and out on time are absolutely essential.

Everyone knows the rules for a nice restaurant:
1. You call ahead for reservations.
2. Upon arrival, you give the host/hostess your name and wait to be seated.
3. A waiter delivers a menu to you and may place a napkin in your lap.
4. And soon ...

Everyone knows ... except the autistic individual!

Figure 4.1. Power Card and Yu-Gi-Oh!

POWER CARD SCRIPT

Kazuki Takahashi Initiates Conversations That Focus on Others' Interests

Kazuki Takahashi is interested in other people and has learned to talk about things they like. He knows that people like to hear their name, so whenever he greets them, he says their name and looks them in the eye. He usually makes a point of finding out and remembering their special interest or hobby so that he can bring it up in conversation. If the person does not seem very talkative, he will ask a question about their interest and then listen carefully to the reply. Mr. Takahashi will use a key word from the person's reply to make a positive comment.

Kazuki Takahashi knows that people like to talk about their interests. He wants you to use the four steps that will help you have good conversations:

1. Greet the person by name and look them in the eye.
2. Ask about their interest and wait for response.
3. Ask a question about their interest and listen for a key word in their reply.
4. Comment on the interest using the key word.

Put this strategy to use and find out Kazuki's secret to enjoying conversations.

POWER CARD

Kazuki Takahashi talks about other's interests

1. Greet the person by name.
2. Ask about their interest and wait.
3. Ask a question about their interest and listen for the key word.
4. Comment using the key word.

From "Power Cards to Improve Conversation Skills in Adolescents With Asperger Syndrome," by K. M. Davis, R. T. Boon, D. F. Cihak, & C. Fore III, 2010, Focus on Autism and Developmental Disorders, *25, 12-22. Copyright 2010 by Sage. Used with permission.*

Every environment has a hidden curriculum—the unwritten rules—the do's and don'ts that are not spelled out but that everyone somehow knows (LaVoie 1994; Myles, Endow, & Mayfield, 2013). The hidden curriculum includes idioms, metaphors, slang, multiple meaning words, nonliteral phrases, expectations, pleasing behaviors, whom to interact with and whom to stay away from, behaviors that attract negative or positive attention and more. Understanding the hidden curriculum can make a huge difference in the lives of autistic people. It can keep them out of trouble and help them make friends.

Many words, phrases, rules, and guidelines used by the neuromajority are tricky and sometimes seem nonsensical. They are definitely not literal. For many autistic people, the hidden curriculum can be problematic. Its meaning is not clear, and it is not taught but is assumed knowledge. The following figures provide a brief insight into the hidden curriculum and why it is difficult for autistic people to understand.

Figure 4.2. I Give Weird Hints

Figure 4.3. A Quote from David Burge

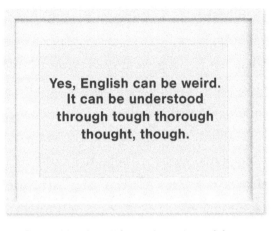

Retrieved from https://ifunny.co/picture/yes-english-can-be-weird-it-can-be-understood-through-E4fn6TZAA

Amal, a rule-following student, became very upset when her teacher told the class that they needed to "buckle down and get to work." She could not figure out what she was supposed to buckle down and became very upset because she wanted to do what the teacher wanted.

Autistics are at a disadvantage because they usually do not understand the hidden curriculum and, therefore, inadvertently break the rules associated with it. As a result, they either get in trouble, become ostracized, or are hurt by peers.

Direct instruction is required. They need to be taught, for example, that some middle school students curse but that most kids don't curse in front of an adult. Autistic adults need to know that even though they do not personally like their boss, they always speak to them with respect. And so on. Teaching the hidden curriculum is strongest when context (Vermeulen, 2012) and prediction (Vermeulen, 2023) is included in instruction. For example, when teaching the hidden curriculum item, "Acceptable slang that may be used with your peers (e.g., dawg, phat) may not be acceptable when interacting with adults," ask learners (a) where and when this item may be true or false (context) and (b) what would happen if slang were used with a principal, police officer, college admissions officer, or human resources officer conducting an interview (prediction).

Temple Grandin, the internationally known author and speaker, developed her own set of rules to guide her social interactions and behavior in society. Many of them are from the hidden curriculum (see Table 4.3).

Who should teach the hidden curriculum? Anyone who supports the autistic individual. There are many hidden curriculum items, such as how to interact with other students and adults at school, that teachers can comfortably teach and should teach as they would reading, writing, or social studies. There are other hidden curriculum items, such as understanding the rules associated with dating and developing intimate relationships, about which peers and familiar adults should provide instruction. Table 4.4 provides a sample list of hidden curriculum items.

Acting Lessons

Many autistic adults suggest that acting lessons are an effective means of teaching self-regulation and social understanding. During acting lessons, they learn to express verbally and nonverbally their emotions in specific situations. They also learn to interpret others' emotions, feelings, and voices. Perhaps more important, in acting class, participants engage in simulations and receive direct and immediate feedback from an instructor and peers regarding their performance.

Table 4.3. Temple Grandin's Rule System to Guide Her Social Interactions and Behavior

1. **Really Bad Things**—Examples: murder, arson, stealing, lying in court under oath, injuring or hitting other people. All cultures have prohibitions against really bad things because an orderly, civilized society cannot function if people are robbing and killing each other.

2. **Courtesy Rules**—Do not cut in on a line at the movie theater or airport. Observe table manners, say thank you, and keep yourself clean. These things are important because they make the other people around you more comfortable. I don't like it when somebody else has sloppy table manners, so I try to have decent table manners. It annoys me if somebody cuts in front of me in a line, so I do not do this to other people.

3. **Illegal But Not Bad**—Examples: slight speeding on the freeway and illegal parking. However, parking in a handicapped zone would be worse because it would violate the courtesy rules.

4. **Sins of the System (SOS)**—Examples: smoking pot (and being thrown in jail for ten years) and sexual misbehavior. SOSs are things where the penalty is so severe that it defies all logic. Sometimes, the penalty for sexual misbehavior is worse than killing somebody. Rules governing sexual behavior are so emotionally based that I do not dare discuss the subject for fear of committing an SOS. An SOS in one society may be acceptable behavior in another, whereas rules 1, 2, 3 tend to be more uniform between different cultures. I have never done a sin of the system ... People with autism have to learn that certain behaviors will not be tolerated—period. You will be fired no matter how good your work is if you commit an SOS at work. People with autism and Asperger's need to learn that if they want to keep a job, they must not commit an SOS ... The social knowledge required is just too complex.

Grandin, T. "Learning Social Rules," Autism Asperger's Digest, *January/February 2005.*

Table 4.4. Sample Hidden Curriculum Items

- Treat all authority figures (e.g., police, firefighters) with respect. You would not address a police officer like you would your brother.
- Not all people you are unfamiliar with are strangers you cannot trust. You may not know your bus driver or your police officer, but these are people who help you.
- What may be acceptable at your house may not be acceptable at a friend's house. For example, although it is acceptable to put your feet up on the table at home, your friend's mom may be upset if you do that in their home.
- People do not always want to know the truth even when they ask. Your best friend does not want to hear that she looks fat in a new dress she just bought for a special occasion.
- It is impolite to interrupt someone talking unless it is an emergency.
- Acceptable slang that may be used with your peers (e.g., dawg, phat) may not be acceptable when interacting with adults.
- If you wish to keep your job, you must be nice to your boss or supervisor even if you do not like them.
- When a teacher tells another student to stop talking, it is not an appropriate time for you to start talking to your neighbor.

Myles, B. S., Trautman, M. L., & Schelvan, R. L. (2013). The Hidden Curriculum: Practical Solutions for Understanding Unstated Rules in Social Situations (2nd ed.). *Arllington, TX: Future Horizons.*

One autistic adult, Margo, credits her success in expressing emotions and interpreting social situations to acting lessons. She acknowledges that her "real-life" performances may be a bit stilted, but after taking acting classes she understands better how to act and react in a neuromajority world.

Self-Esteem Building

Autistic individuals may act different, feel different, and, in some ways, be different from others. They often know this, and, sadly, loss of self-esteem is frequently the byproduct. For adults, there is a high price to pay for a negative self-esteem. It has been documented that autistic adults have higher levels of depression, anxiety, suicide, and other affective disorders than the general population, which can partially be related to their self-concept (cf. Dell'Osso et al., 2019).

Support persons must help autistics to understand that they are more than their exceptionality. Yes, they have an exceptionality, but this is only one part of them. They have many characteristics that must be pointed out and celebrated (cf. Bury et al., 2020; Clark & Adams, 2020). Positive aspects of autism along with other strengths should be emphasized. The individual should understand that all people are special. Everyone is able to do certain things well, while other tasks are challenging. The following is a list of resources that reinforce the idea that autistics have many strengths and unique talents.

Multimedia Lessons

Most autistic individuals are visual learners, so interventions that use the visual modality are often especially effective. One such intervention is videos. In addition to their visual format, videos offer several advantages. For example, (a) they show skills in a fluid format so that they can be seen as a whole instead of as a set of discrete steps, (b) they are often motivating because of their pace and content, and (c) they allow for multiple viewings to ensure that learners acquire the skill that is targeted.

Three video-based strategies—video modeling, video detective, and vintage videos—are discussed below.

Video Modeling

Using video self-modeling, individuals learn to interact with others by observing themselves or others on videotape engaging in an interaction.

One type of video self-modeling is *positive self-review*. The individual is taped when engaging in a behavior, and the video is used as a reminder to engage in that behavior. Positive self-review is best employed when the learner has developed a specific social skill but is either (a) not using it at the appropriate level because it is newly acquired, or (b) not maintaining it in the natural environment (Debar et al., 2022).

Another type of video self-modeling is *feedforward*. This approach is used when somebody has learned individual skills but cannot put them together and use them in a real-life situation. In addition, it can assist in transferring skills across environments (Egarr & Storey, 2021).

> JaeWook had learned all the steps for approaching and talking with a colleague during lunch, but when given the opportunity to use these skills, he would freeze after merely saying hello. To help him use the skills, his job coach videotaped JaeWook engaging in the steps he had learned to use and edited the tape so that it showed all the individual steps sequentially. When JaeWook saw the videotape, he was able to transfer the interaction skills during lunch.

Video Detective

In another example of how to use videotapes, one mother teaches her son about nonverbal communication through the television series *Blue Bloods* and *The Big Bang Theory*. After she has introduced a concept, she plays the television show with the sound turned down and asks her son to predict the actors' nonverbal and verbal communication messages based on what he sees on the screen.

Similarly, a facilitator of an adult social skills group routinely videotapes participants during planned simulations and regular activities and uses the videos as instructional tools. This allows the autistic adults to see themselves giving mixed messages or using effective verbal strategies to communicate to others, and also to monitor their voice tone or proximity. The facilitator also works with small groups to create scripts that the adults act out on video. She plays the videotaped scripts and hosts two game show-type activities for her contestants, "What's My Emotion?" and "Find the Conversation Flaw."

Vintage Videos

Vintage videos can be excellent teaching tools. For example, silent Charlie Chaplin and Buster Keaton movies offer opportunities to view facial expressions and link them with situations without having to navigate through spoken language. Similarly, the character Lucy Ricardo of the television show *I Love Lucy* offers exaggerated facial expressions that can also be helpful in teaching social understanding.

Instruction for the Support Person

Adults must know how to support the individual who experiences meltdowns and make plans accordingly. Such knowledge and preparation will help ensure that if a meltdown occurs, it can be addressed in a manner that will minimize student distress (Myles & Simpson, 1999).

The following is a series of steps that can be taken both as preventive measures and as actions during a meltdown. Adults who support the autistic individual must be trained on what to do during the Cycle of Meltdowns.

Dress for Possible Meltdowns

Adults who support students who experience meltdowns should dress in a manner that will not interfere with their ability to appropriately respond to student needs. For example, wearing low-heeled shoes and loose-fitting garments, avoiding sharp jewelry and dangling earrings, and choosing short hair styles or wearing hair pulled back may increase the effectiveness of the adult responding to children and youth who experience the Cycle of Meltdowns.

Keep Items of Value Away from Children and Youth Who Experience Meltdowns

During the cycle, autistics may to attempt to destroy items important to their teachers. Such items should be removed from the classroom or kept away from students who may have melt-downs. Remember: this behavior is not purposeful or planned. Think of the individual as operating on "automatic pilot."

Establish Trust and Rapport with Students

Autistic children and youth know when their teachers like and enjoy them. This relationship, while not meltdowns, may reduce their occurrence. Therefore, it is imperative that adults let students know that they are liked and valued.

Remain Calm During Meltdowns

The ability to remain calm can be learned with practice and experience. Because students are not available for learning during the Cycle of Meltdowns, adults should acknowledge that their words are often not processed during the process. During the cycle, many adults talk to students to (a) let students know by their tone of voice that they are supporting the child and (b) keep themselves calm. Adults should not threaten children and youth. Rather, children should be calmly told rules and consequences and what they need to do to end the cycle (e.g., "As soon as you are quietly seated, we can discuss this.").

Adults should also communicate that autistic individuals are permitted to be upset and angry in an appropriate manner (this is best not taught when the child is in the Cycle of Meltdowns). That is, when autistic students are in the "Ready to Learn" mode, adults should teach that everyone becomes upset and that it is okay to become angry, but anger needs to be expressed in an appropriate way. Finally, adults should not argue with students but accept the fact that they will not win arguments with them once the cycle has started. Once a power struggle begins, the adult has already lost. It is much more productive to acknowledge students' feelings ("It's okay to be angry—sit down and we can talk about it."), ignore accusations, and assertively focus on steps needed to move the child to the recovery stage and ultimately to the teachable moment.

Finally, adults who work or live with autistics who experience meltdowns should be reminded that their job is to assist these individuals in acquiring skills and knowledge that will assist them in the future. That is, adults need to be active instructors—using the teachable moment to help students learn how to recognize that they are upset, how to express this behavior, and how to self-calm.

Interpretation

Interpretation refers to the recognition that, no matter how well-developed their skills, situations will arise that autistic persons and support personnel do not understand. In addition to confusion, this may result in extreme stress, which may lead to the Cycle of Meltdowns. To help prevent this from happening, someone in the environment must serve as an interpreter using a variety of techniques to help to explain the social environment.

Interpretation for the Autistic Individual

It is essential to support autistic individuals in assigning meaning to their emotions, sensations, and behaviors. It is equally important that autistics understand others' emotions, sensations, and behaviors. Interpretation strategies that facilitate understanding include:

a. rating scales   c. cartooning

b. sensory awareness   d. social autopsies

Each is discussed below.

Rating Scales

Behavior regulation includes the ability to read and self-monitor positive and negative reactions as well as to understand elements in the environment that may cause discomfort. As mentioned, autistic individuals often have difficulty interpreting their emotions and social well-being. This is not because they are avoiding an uncomfortable situation or misleading themselves or others, but because they often cannot tell what they are feeling. In addition, autistic individuals have difficulty self-calming (Mahler, 2019). Therefore, it is important to provide strategies that will help them to understand their emotions and to respond appropriately. Two rating scales address this important topic.

Stress-Tracking Thermometer: McAfee's (2013) stress-tracking thermometer from Navigating the Social World works well with autistics. Through the use of a Stress Thermometer, autistics learn to:

- Identify and label their emotions using nonverbal and situational cues
- Assign appropriate values to different degrees of emotion, such as anger
- Redirect negative thoughts to positive thoughts
- Identify environmental stressors and common reactions to them
- Recognize the early signs of stress
- Select relaxation techniques that match their needs

A sample Stress Thermometer appears in Figure 4.4.

Figure 4.4. Stress Thermometer.

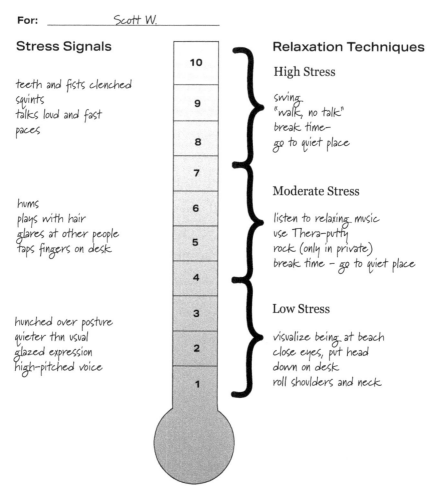

For: _____Scott W._____

Stress Signals

teeth and fists clenched
squints
talks loud and fast
paces

hums
plays with hair
glares at other people
taps fingers on desk

hunched over posture
quieter thn usual
glazed expression
high-pitched voice

Relaxation Techniques

High Stress

swing
"walk, no talk"
break time-
go to quiet place

Moderate Stress

listen to relaxing music
use Thera-putty
rock (only in private)
break time - go to quiet place

Low Stress

visualize being at beach
close eyes, put head
down on desk
roll shoulders and neck

From McAfee, J. (2013). Navigating the Social World: A Curriculum for Individuals with Asperger's Syndrome, High Functioning Autism and Related Disorders *(p. 47). Arlington, TX: Future Horizons, Inc. Reprinted with permission.*

The Incredible 5-Point Scale: Incredible 5-Point Scale books have been developed to help autistic children as well as adolescents and adults (Buron & Curtis, 2022) to understand themselves and therefore better regulate their behavior. The scale is unique in that it has a wide range of applications. It can be used as an obsessional index, a stress scale, a meltdown monitor, and so on. Individuals learn to recognize the stages of their specific behavioral challenges and methods to self-calm at each level. The Incredible 5-Point Scale identifies, in the individual's own words, (a) a term to describe her behavior at 1, 2, etc.; (b) what the behavior feels like at each number; and (c) what she can do to address the behavior at each level. Figures 4.5 and 4.6 provide illustrations of how the Incredible 5-Point Scale may be used.

Figure 4.5. The Obsessional Index

Kevin is in the fifth grade. He is autistic and has obsessive compulsive disorder. Kevin loves balls and will go to great lengths to find a ball and throw it on top of the highest available ledge or roof. The ball-throwing becomes a problem when he hurts others to get at a ball or when he runs through the school with a ball trying to find a high ledge. His anxiety over ball throwing is so intense that his thinking becomes illogical.

The following is Kevin's account of his ball obsession, which he reported to his teacher when she interviewed him as a part of a functional behavior assessment:

"I don't want to be obsessed with balls or balloons. It is a stupid obsession. I can't be the boss of anything. I want to be back to being a baby again. Maybe then I could start over. When I go to people's houses, I steal their balls, and that's embarrassing. No one in the neighborhood understands me. I hate obsessions. They make me mad. I really want to get rid of them but I can't. I can't do anything right. Every time I see a ball, I have to have it. I know right from wrong, but this is just too hard."

The 5-Point Scale was designed to teach Kevin how to recognize his need for support in dealing with his obsessions before it was too late. On some days, he didn't even seem to think about balls; in fact, on those days his obsessive personality seemed to help him to stay focused on his work. On other days, he would think about balls, but it didn't seem to bother him much. On those days, he was so relaxed that he could handle his thoughts about balls. Some days he just wanted to talk about his obsession with balls. If the adult with him told him not to talk about it, it often led to increased anxiety and acting-out behavior. Some days Kevin would come off the bus already talking rapidly about balls, types of balls, sizes of balls, and so on. We knew that on those days, he was going to need added support. This support often meant that Kevin did his work outside of the classroom to lower his anxiety about "blowing it" in front of the other kids.

Kevin had refused social stories in the past because he thought they were for "babies." Instead, we wrote him a memo to explain the new scale idea. Kevin loved the memo and kept it with him. He checked in with the special education teacher each morning to rate himself, and within a month he was accurately rating his anxiety about balls.

After we introduced the memo to him, there have only been a few days when Kevin had to work outside of the classroom for most of the day because his anxiety was high. Although he continues to have occasional rough days, he has not had to leave the classroom since we started the program.

MEMO

To: Kevin

Re: When Your Obsessions Get Too Big

Sometimes having obsessions can be a positive thing, because it means that your brain is capable of latching onto an idea and not letting go. This can be beneficial for great explorers, inventors and writers. BUT sometimes having obsessions can be very upsetting and frustrating.

This memo is to inform you that I understand that sometimes your obsessions get so big that you are not able to control them because of the severe level of anxiety they cause. It would be highly beneficial for you to learn to tell the difference between when your obsessions are too big to handle and when they are feeling more like positive obsessions. One way to do this is to do a "check-in" three times a day when you consider your obsessional index. The first step is to help me fill out the following chart by rating your obsessional index on a 1-5 rating scale. Thank you for your cooperation.

Kari Dunn Buron

From Buron, K. D., & Curtis, M. (2022). The Incredible 5-Point Scale 2nd Edition Revised. Saint Paul, MN: 5 Point Scale Publishing (pp. 25–27). Reprinted with permission.

Figure 4.6. "I'm 6'2", Strong as an Ox – So Can You Tell Me Why I'm Trembling?"

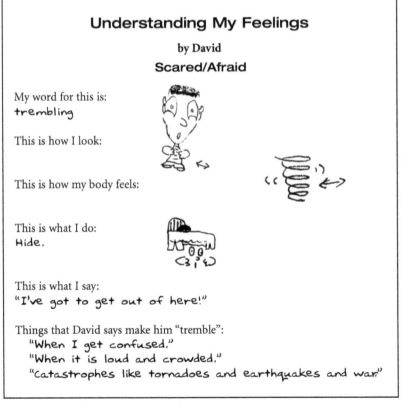

"I'm 6'2", Strong as an Ox – So Can You Tell Me Why I'm Trembling?"

David was referred to the self-contained high school program after being expelled from his home high school. He had broken several windows in the school cafeteria and the glass entrance/exit door nearest to the cafeteria. As a result, he had been to juvenile court and was placed on probation.

David identified his behavior as self-defense. "It was like my head was going to explode because of all the noise and confusion in the cafeteria. It's always confusing, and today there was a food fight. I had to do something to make it stop, I was afraid my head was going to explode."

The rating scale that follows does not rate David's level of anger, but his fear. David told us he feels afraid when he is "confused" so when developing this scale, we discussed things that we were afraid of, and David drew pictures to help him understand his own fear.

Understanding My Feelings

by David
Scared/Afraid

My word for this is:
trembling

This is how I look:

This is how my body feels:

This is what I do:
Hide.

This is what I say:
"I've got to get out of here!"

Things that David says make him "tremble":
"When I get confused."
"When it is loud and crowded."
"Catastrophes like tornadoes and earthquakes and war."

Name: David _____ My Scared/Afraid/Trembling Scale

Rating	Looks/Sounds like	Feels like	Safe people can help / I can try to
5	Wide-eyed, maybe screaming, and running, hitting.	I am going to explode if I don't do something.	I will need an adult to help me leave. Help!
4	Threaten others or bump them.	People are talking about me. I feel irritated, mad.	Close my mouth and hum. Squeeze my hands. Leave the room for a walk.
3	You can't tell I'm scared. Jaw clenched.	I shiver inside.	Write or draw about it. Close my eyes.
2	I still look normal.	My stomach gets a little queasy.	Slow my breathing. Tell somebody safe how I feel.
1	Normal— you can't tell by looking at me.	I don't know, really.	Enjoy it!

From Buron, K. D., & Curtis, M. (2022). The Incredible 5-Point Scale 2nd edition revised. Saint Paul, MN: 5 Point Scale Publishing (pp. 25–27, 50–52). Reprinted with permission.

Sensory Awareness

All of the information we receive from our environment comes through the sensory system. Taste, smell, sight, sound, touch, movement, the force of gravity, body position, and internal sensations are the basic sensory ingredients that enable all individuals to listen, attend for a period of time, and be calm enough or awake enough to participate in learning experiences and other daily activities (cf. Mahler, 2019).

Those who interact with autistics often assume that they have an intact sensory system, but this is not always the case (Marco, Hinkley, Hill, & Nagarajan, 2001). In fact, autistic individuals often have one or more areas of the sensory system that is over-reactive, under-reactive, or alternately over- and under-reactive.

A sensory diet is one way to provide sensory-based activities selected to address the specific needs of an individual (e.g., movement, touch, auditory). Activities are provided in a systematic, prescriptive manner (Pingale et al., 2019). With the assistance of an occupational therapist who is knowledgeable about sensory functioning, individuals can be taught how to understand their sensory systems and to incorporate sensory strategies into their daily activities to help them to remain regulated and to reduce the risk of entering the Cycle of Meltdowns.

Mahler (2022) created *The Interoception Curriculum: A Step By Step Framework for Developing Mindful Self-Regulation*. As previously discussed, interoception is the ability to notice and connect bodily sensations with emotions. Some experience interoceptive signals that are so strong, they are immediately overwhelmed and confused. Others experience dulled or muted interoception signals that leave them unable to respond until they reach a fever pitch. This can lead to significant difficulties with emotional regulation and managing challenging behavior. This curriculum provides a systematic, guided process to develop and build interoceptive awareness.

Cartooning

Visual symbols, such as schedules and cartoons, have been found to enhance an understanding of the environment. For example, research has shown that visual support can serve as an effective means of teaching educational, functional living, and social skills (cf. Watkins et al., 2019).

One type of visual support is cartooning. The technique of cartooning, used as a generic term, has been implemented by speech-language pathologists for many years to enhance their clients' understanding, including illustrating the meaning of idioms, understanding the sequence of events, and interpreting social situations. Used in more specific ways, cartooning has played an integral role in several intervention techniques such as pragmaticism (Arwood, Brown, & Kaulitz, 2015) and *Comic Strip Conversations*^{TM} (Gray, 1994).

Cartooning promotes social understanding by incorporating simple figures and other symbols in a comic strip format. Speech, thought bubble symbols, and sometimes color are used to help the individual see and analyze a situation. Support persons can draw a social situation to facilitate understanding or assist the autistic person in creating his own illustrations. It is not necessary to be a skillful artist to draw cartoons!

Cartooning strategies have been refined by Arwood et al. They call the cartoon a "form of visual language" and "story telling in picture form" (p. 1). According to these authors, cartooning is used to:

- Explain and change behavior
- Improve social skills
- Manage time
- Improve academic skills
- Help students clarify or refine their ideas

Arwood, Brown, and Kaulitz offer guidelines for how to draw cartoons, including (a) using connected frames to illustrate sequence, (b) grounding the characters within the cartoon so that there is no air between the person and the ground, and (c) making the drawn ideas move in one direction only. Figure 4.7 shows an example of a cartoon for social change—*Mark wants to make friends, but he stands too close to other students.*

Figure 4.7. Sample Cartoon

From A Guide to Cartooning and Flowcharting (p. 3), by Ellyn Lucas Arwood, Ed.D., CCC-SLP, and Mabel M. Brown, M.A., 1999. Apricot, Inc. Used with permission.

Social Autopsies

Developed by LaVoie (1994) to help individuals understand social mistakes and social successes, a social autopsy is used to dissect social incidents so that individuals learn from experiences. Social autopsies are particularly well-suited to interpreting social and behavioral situations. After an event, the individual and the support person analyze the components of a social situation, identifying correct and incorrect actions or words. If an error was made, together they develop a plan to ensure that it does not reoccur.

Because of the visual strengths of most autistic persons, social autopsies may be enhanced by adding written words, phrases, or pictorial representations to events. Lavoie overviewed the attributes and nonattributes of social autopsies, reiterating that it is a supportive, interpretive technique (see Table 4.5).

Table 4.5. Attributes and Nonattributes of Social Autopsies

A social autopsy is ...	A social autopsy is not ...
• Supportive, structure, constructive	• Punishment
• Solution-oriented	• Negative
• An opportunity for the autistic individual to participate	• Controlled by a support person
• A process for interpretation	• A "one-time" solution
• Conducted after a social error or social success	
• Led by an adult significant to the autistic individual	
• Generally held in a 1-on-1 session	

Interpretation for the Support Person

The support person must be able to quickly interpret behaviors that indicates that the autistic individual is in distress—that is, when they are in the Rumbling Stage. It is equally important that support persons understand behaviors associated with the Rage and Recovery Stages as well as associated interventions.

The Student Crisis Plan Sheet, an easy-to-use tool that can facilitate interpretation, is often developed as a part of an individualized education program (IEP) and/or behavior intervention plan (BIP). It is helpful in ensuring that everyone involved is following the same plan to help the autistic individual exert positive control over their environment.

Figure 4.8 provides a copy of this form for school-aged individuals; Figure 4.9 addresses meltdowns that may occur in a home- or center-based daycare setting.

Figure 4.8. Student Crisis Plan Sheet for School-Age Individuals

Student Crisis Plan Sheet

Student Name _____ Student Age/Grade _____

Teacher Name _____ Date of Plan _____

ENVIRONMENTAL/PERSONNEL CONSIDERATIONS

1. Describe how you can obtain assistance when it is needed _____
_____
_____

2. At which stage should outside assistance be sought?

_____ rumbling _____ rage _____ recovery

3. Which school personnel are available to provide assistance?

_____ principal _____ school psychologist _____ paraprofessional
_____ social worker _____ counselor
_____ other (please specify) _____
_____ other (please specify) _____

4. Where should child(ren) exit to? (specify room or school) _____

5. At what stage should the plan be used by others in the classroom?

_____ rumbling _____ rage _____ recovery

6. Are there any extenuating circumstances that others should know about this student (i.e., medications, related medical conditions, home situation)?

7. Who should be notified of the incident? _____

8. How should the incident be documented? _____

RUMBLING STAGE

1. What environmental factors/activities or antecedents lead to "rumbling" behaviors?

_____ unplanned change   _____ difficult assignment   _____ crowds
_____ teacher criticism   _____ transitions   _____ conflict with classmate
_____ other (please describe) _____

2. What behaviors does the student exhibit during the rumbling stage?

_____ bites nails   _____ tenses muscles   _____ stares
_____ taunts others   _____ refuses to work   _____ fidgets
_____ other (please describe) _____
_____ other (please describe) _____

3. Does the student mention any of the following complaints or illness?

_____ stomachache   _____ headache   _____ not applicable
_____ other (please describe) _____

4. Should the student be sent to the nurse if there is a complaint of illness?

_____ yes   _____ no

5. How long does the rumbling stage last before it progresses to the next stage?

_____

6. What interventions should be used at this stage?

_____ antiseptic bouncing   _____ proximity control   _____ touch control
_____ "just walk and don't talk"   _____ home base   _____ redirecting
_____ other (please specify) _____
_____
_____ other (please specify) _____
_____

RAGE STAGE

1. What behaviors does the student exhibit during the rage stage?

_____ student verbally lashes out at teacher   _____ student verbally lashes out at other students

_____ student threatens to hit teacher   _____ student threatens to hit students

_____ student destroys materials   _____ student attempts to leave classroom

_____ student withdraws from teacher   _____ student hurts self

_____ other (please specify) _____

_____ other (please specify) _____

2. What teacher interventions should be used during this stage?

_____ physically move child to safe room   _____ prompt child to move to safe room

_____ remove others from the classroom   _____ redirect student

_____ other (please specify) _____

_____ other (please specify) _____

3. What is the role of others in the child's environment during the rage stage?_____

_____

_____

RECOVERY STAGE

1. What behaviors does the student exhibit during the recovery stage without intervention?

_____ sullenness   _____ withdrawal into fantasy   _____ denial

_____ "typical" student behavior

_____ other (please describe) _____

_____ other (please describe) _____

2. What supportive techniques should be used during this stage?_____

_____

_____

3. What interventions should be used at a later time to assist the student in gaining more self-control?_____

_____

_____

Figure 4.9. Child Crisis Plan Sheet for Home and Center-Based Daycare Settings

Child Crisis Plan Sheet

Child Name ———————————————— Child Age ——————

Provider/Teacher ————————————— Date of Plan ——————

ENVIRONMENTAL/PERSONNEL CONSIDERATIONS

Describe how you can get assistance. ————————————————

————————————————————————————

At which stage should help be sought? ——————————————

————————————————————————————

Who can provide help? ———————————————————

What should other children do?————————————————

Have other children practiced what to do so their action are automatic?   Yes ☐ No ☐

How you set up the environment to manage a meltdown for the child and their peers?

————————————————————————————

————————————————————————————

————————————————————————————

Are there any circumstances about the child that are important to know (i.e., medication, medical conditions, home circumstances)?

————————————————————————————

Who should be notified of the situation?

————————————————————————————

How should the situation be documented?

————————————————————————————

RUMBLING STAGE

What factors lead to rumbling behavior?

☐ Unplanned change   ☐ Conflict with peer
☐ Difficult activity   ☐ Redirection/ correction
☐ Transition
☐ Other (please describe)

_____

_____

What behaviors does the child exhibit during the rumbling stage?

☐ Stares   ☐ Tenses muscles
☐ Fidgets   ☐ Tears up
☐ Whines   ☐ Stomachache/illness
☐ Other (please describe)

_____

_____

_____

If another adult is present, what should that adult do?

_____

_____

How long does the rumbling stage usually last?

_____

What interventions should be used during this stage?

☐ Support from routine   ☐ Antiseptic bouncing
☐ Home base   ☐ Change order of activities
☐ Acknowledge child difficulties   ☐ Self-calming
☐ Read a social narrative   ☐ Just walk and don't talk
☐ Other

_____

_____

RAGE STAGE

What behaviors does the child exhibit during the rage stage?

☐ Biting   ☐ Crying
☐ Hitting   ☐ Destroys materials
☐ Kicking   ☐ Internalizes behavior/freezes
☐ Other

What interventions should be used during the rage stage?

☐ Move child to home base   ☐ Remove other children
☐ Redirect to another activity
☐ Other

If another adult is present, what should that adult do?

RECOVERY STAGE

What behaviors does the child exhibit during the recovery stage

☐ Sleeps   ☐ Withdraws
☐ Other   ☐ Cries

What supportive interventions should be used during this stage?

☐ Known calming strategies   ☐ Activities that include a
☐ Provide structure   special interest
☐ Easy activities
☐ Other

What skills can the student be taught to decrease the cycle of meltdowns?

Coaching

Coaching, the third element in this multifaceted approach to intervention, recognizes that while some autistic individuals and support persons know how to use a specific skill, they may not use it when appropriate. This may occur for a variety of reasons, including (a) difficulty generalizing the strategy to different settings, situations, and people; (b) experiencing a high level of stress that may cause the individual to temporarily "forget" the skills or not being able to recall the skills in the moment; and (c) forgetting how to begin the first step in the strategy.

Coaching for the Autistic Person

Coaching helps an autistic person grow and develop their skills. Often, coaching provides a "jump start" for the autistic person. Coaching may take many forms. For example, a support person may:

- **Prompt.** Prompt an individual to take a deep breath or a short break when things are getting difficult.
- **Narrate.** Point out someone at a social event who is alone and who might want to interact socially. *"Marcus is standing over there by himself. I think that he might want someone to play with. Why don't you go over and talk to him?"* Note that the coach did not simply suggest *what* to do but also provided a *why*.
- **Suggest.** Provide the adult with a sentence or topic to use in a social exchange. *"Ask Libby if she has seen [the latest superhero movie]. If she has, you can say, 'What did you like about the movie?' If she says that she hasn't seen the movie, say, 'What movies have you seen lately?'"*

- **Provide the Set-Up.** Some autistic individuals become highly anxious when they attempt to enter a conversation or other social interaction. In some cases, this anxiety is enough to trigger the meltdown cycle. The coach provides a sentence or phrase to begin the conversation, such as *"We are going to the store and John has something to ask you before we go."*

- **Signal.** Coaching may also include nonverbal cues. These simple cues may provide the support and encouragement the person needs in order to participate in the interaction rather than entering the rumbling stage. For example, a coach and an autistic person might have a prearranged, discrete signal that cues the person to change topics, ask a question of a communicative partner, or move away from or toward someone. Subtle signals include touching an earlobe or clearing the throat. When selecting a signal, the support person must first ensure that the signal is readily noticeable to the individual but not to others in the environment. A second consideration is ensuring that the signal is not distracting. If the individual looks intently for the signal, he may not be able to engage in a conversation with a peer. In this case, the signal becomes more important than the social interaction and, therefore, is counterproductive.

Coaching for the Support Person

Coaching can be beneficial when support personnel are learning any new skill. Two important areas for coaching are described below:

    a. practicing for a meltdown

    b. changing countercontrol behaviors.

Practicing for a Meltdown

Adults should be prepared for a meltdown. For example, they should know (a) where to go during times when students have meltdowns (i.e., what exits to use, where in the room to go); (b) who should be notified, how these contacts will occur, who will make the contacts, etc.; (c) what students not involved in the rage cycle should do during these occurrences; and (d) roles of other adults during the stages of the cycle. If the support person is observed during the Cycle of Meltdowns, the coaching and feedback they receive will help them become more efficient and confident in addressing meltdowns. When accompanied by instruction and written plans that identify adult roles, interventions to be used at each stage of the cycle, and evaluation methods, coaching is a strong and effective intervention.

Stopping Behaviors That Prompt Countercontrol

The concept of countercontrol is important to understand when supporting autistics who experience the Cycle of Meltdowns. Many autistic individuals do not cope well when faced with control by adults, so they may try to countercontrol. That is, autistic individuals may take steps (sometimes subconsciously) to be in control. According to Carey and Bourbon (2004),

... behaviors that are problematic for people who work with children might be countercontrol in disguise. When people describe a child's behavior with certain words—*noncompliant, disobedient, resistant, willful, persistent, stubborn, oppositional, rebellious*—countercontrol may be lurking. In fact, any time a student's behavior frustrates your attempts to see that student acting in a particular way, you could be experiencing countercontrol. (p. 4)

Note. While Carey and Bourbon discuss countercontrol in children and students, it can occur with individuals of all ages and across settings.

The more adults try to control, the more some autistics try to countercontrol. The following tends to promote countercontrol behaviors: (a) tightening reinforcement contingencies, (b) introducing time-out, and (c) assuming more stringent punishments.

Countercontrol is minimized when individuals perceive they have choices and understand why they are learning specific skills. Another effective control measure is to incorporate special into the curriculum. Compromise and negotiation opportunities also lessen the occurrence of countercontrol. Carey and Bourbon (2004) pose three questions that support persons should ask to help determine if they are too controlling:

1. When you are teaching, do you ever get frustrated or angry?
2. With some students, do you find that the more you try to direct them, the more difficult they become?

3. Do you sometimes feel like students are manipulating you and that they often seem to enjoy seeing you become upset? (pp. 8–9)

Affirmative responses to these questions may mean that adults working or living with an autistic individual may be too controlling and, therefore, need to reduce their controlling behaviors. This will, in turn, reduce countercontrol in students.

Changing controlling behaviors is difficult. Sometimes a support person may not be aware that they are using control as a strategy and/or the controlling behavior is engrained in the support person's daily functioning. Either way, coaching provides direct feedback and support for those who wish to be more effective in helping autistic people.

Obstacle Removal

Finally, obstacle removal, the fourth component of effective programming, involves modifying tasks and the environment to overcome barriers to understanding, learning, and performing a task or activity. Problems arise when an obstacle is in the path. "Solving a problem directly generated by an obstacle rarely works because, in many cases, the obstacle is still there" (Samuel, 2019, 1). It is essential to find a way to remove the obstacle itself.

Obstacle Removal for the Autistic Person

Ideally, the individual will learn over the years to remove obstacles in their environment (or request that they be removed) when possible or to compensate for the presence of the obstacle so that they can continue to participate successfully. Obstacle removal includes the use of visual, peer, and environmental supports.

As mentioned, most autistic individuals benefit from information that is presented visually rather than auditorily because it is more concrete and allows for greater processing time. The following describes essential visual supports for all learners—autistics and neuromajority peers:

a. visual schedules

b. posted rules

c. routine cards

d. voice volume scale

e. problem-solving scale

f. check-in chat

g. cool zone/home base/break card

h. make-another-choice card

i. visual boundaries, and graphic organizers

Visual Schedules

Visual schedules, such as the one shown in Figure 4.7, present an abstract concept such as time in a more concrete and manageable form. As such, visual schedules can yield multiple benefits for autistics. For example, visual schedules allow someone to anticipate upcoming events and activities, develop an understanding of time, and facilitate the ability to predict change. Further, they can be utilized to stimulate communicative exchanges through a discussion of past, present, and future events; increase on-task behavior; facilitate transition between activities; and teach new skills.

Having the autistic individual participate in preparing the schedule is often helpful. For example, a student can assist in assembling his schedule, copying it, or adding his own personal touch in some other manner. This interactive time can also be used to review the daily routine, discuss changes, and review expectations.

Figure 4.10. Penny's Visual Schedule

Penny's Schedule	
Date: <u>Monday, December 8</u> ◈ Means there is a change and that's okay.	
8:00-8:15	Morning routine: ☐ Put away backpack ☐ Turn in homework ☐ Make lunch selection ☐ Take out journal ☐ Check helper chart
8:15-8:30	Write in journal
8:30-9:15	Math
9:15-10:00	Specials (circle one): Music Art P.E.
10:00-10:15	Restroom break
10:15-10:30	Snack and read book
10:30-11:00	Reading/Language Arts
11:00-11:30	Spelling
11:30-12:00	Lunch
12:00-12:30	Recess
12:30-1:00	Speech ◈ Library today because Ms. Jones is out sick
1:00-1:45	Science
1:45-2:15	Social Studies
2:15-2:30	Story time
2:30-2:45	Pack to go home
Thought for the day: Ms. Jones is out today, but that is okay. I will go to the library instead and see Ms. Jones on my speech day when she feels well.	

From Aspy, R., & Grossman, B.G. (2022). The Ziggurat Model: A Framework for Designing Comprehensive Strategies and Supports for Autistic Individuals Release 2.1. *Dallas, TX: The Ziggurat Group. Reprinted with permission.*

Posted Rules

The ability to understand and follow rules is critical to school and life success (Nuske et al., 2019). In addition, when rules are stated positively, taught, and used consistently, autistic individuals experience fewer challenges, including meltdowns (as do their neuromajority peers). Rules should be stated in a manner such that autistics concretely know what to do (see Figure 4.8). For example, rules such as "be safe" can be interpreted many ways, but "Walk down the hallway" communicates what they are supposed to do in a very clearly and concrete manner.

Rules, stated positively, help an individual know what they need to do to fit in and be safe (see Table 4.6). Autistic individuals are likely to respond to positively stated guidelines than to negatively stated ones. When a rule is stated negatively, an individual may not know what to do to get their needs met. For example, a rule that says "No blurting out" does not tell the individual how to get the support person's attention.

Table 4.6. Sample Rules

- Listen to the teacher when they speak.
- Ask for help when you need it
- Bring necessary materials to class: paper, pencil, book, assignment notebook.
- If you want to touch other people's materials, ask first.
- Listen and follow directions.
- Raise your hand before speaking.
- Keep hands, feet, and objects to yourself.

Routine Cards

According to Kathy Quill (personal communication, August 4, 2005), if support persons would spend the first two weeks of the school year teaching routines, students would have fewer challenges. Research supports this: one of the elements of a well-run and emotionally-support classroom is the use of routines (c.f., Rahn et al., 2017).

Routines should be created for commonly occurring activities across the school day. Table 4.7 provides a list of sample routines. A simple guideline: Any regularly occurring direction that begins with "Get ready to" or "Clean out/up" should have a routine card.

Table 4.7. Routines to Teach

How and/or When To:	
• Ask for help	• Line up for various activities
• Obtain forgotten supplies	• Walk down the hall with others
• Sharpen your pencil	• Get ready and move to another activity within the same environment
• Pass out papers	
• Hand in work	• Get ready and move to another activity in a different environment
• Make up missed work	
• Organize materials so that they are accessible in a locker, backpack, desk, or cubby	• Get ready to start the day
	• Get ready to go home
• Clean out locker, backpack, desk, or cubby	• Navigate lunchtime
	• Ask to go to the bathroom

Voice Volume Scale

The Voice Volume Scale is designed to help learners match voice loudness to their many environments. The scale typically contains five levels of volume each with (a) the level number, (b) volume description, (c) picture of the level, and (d) where it is appropriate (see Figure 4.11: Voice Volume Scale).

Not only does this scale allow students to understand voice volume across settings, it allows the support person to change students' voice volume nonverbally by pointing to the appropriate picture on the poster. In many schools, this voice volume is universally adopted so that students see it in the cafeteria, nurse's office, classroom, hallways, administrative offices, library, and other relevant settings.

Figure 4.11. Voice Volume Scale

From Healen, Taylor (March 9, 2020). My Boardmaker Activity. Voice-O-Meter. Retrieved from https://inside.ewu.edu/managementtoolbox/voice-o-meter/.

Problem Solving Rubric

In response to the problem-solving difficulties experienced by those with an autistic neurology (cf. Herrero & Lorenzo, 2020), Mataya and Owens (2013) created the problem-solving scale and curriculum. Using this poster and curriculum, support persons teach learners how to identify a problem and then use the scale to decide how to approach the situation. Typically, solutions include: (a) ignore it and move on, (b) let it bother you, or (c) seek help from an adult. Upper elementary and secondary students learn how to use another problem-solving behavior: (d) talk it out and compromise (see Figure 4.12). Figures 4.13 contains a scale with pictures for nonreaders who have not learned to compromise.

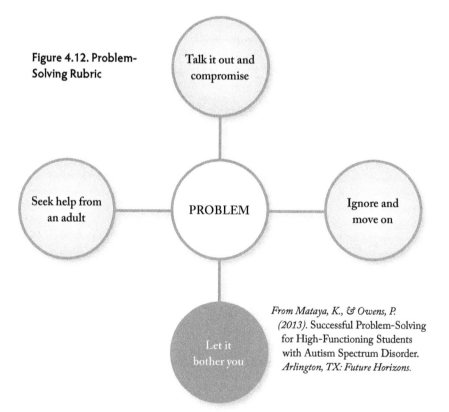

Figure 4.12. Problem-Solving Rubric

Talk it out and compromise

Seek help from an adult

PROBLEM

Ignore and move on

Let it bother you

From Mataya, K., & Owens, P. (2013). Successful Problem-Solving for High-Functioning Students with Autism Spectrum Disorder. *Arlington, TX: Future Horizons.*

Figure 4.13. Problem-Solving Rubric for Nonreaders and/or
Those Who Have Not Learned to Compromise

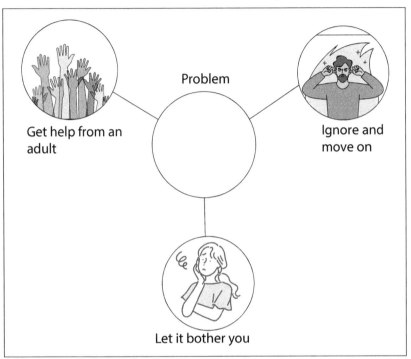

Problem

Get help from an
adult

Ignore and
move on

Let it bother you

Modified from Mataya, K., & Owens, P. (2013). Successful Problem-Solving for High-Functioning Students with Autism Spectrum Disorder. *Arlington, TX: Future Horizons.*

Check-In Chart

As learners enter the classroom or other new environment, they can "sign in" indicating how they are feeling on a five-point scale. They can Velcro™ their name or picture, or write their name on the chart next to their corresponding emotion (see Figure 4.14). This allows the support person, at a glance, to identify those who may need additional support as well as those whose "mood" may not match their report. These learners may need instruction and ongoing support on how to identify their feelings.

Figure 4.14. Check-in Chart.

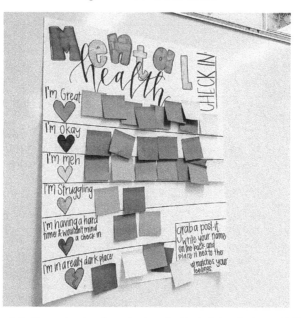

Retrieved from https://www.boredpanda.com/students-health-check-board-erin-castillo/?utm_source= google&utm_medium=organic&utm_campaign=organic.

Cool Zone/Home Base/Break Card

As discussed in Chapter 2, autistics often need a break from their overwhelming environment—whether it be in school, at work, or at home. Having a place where the individual can feel calm and safe can be effective in preventing a meltdown. A sample break card is shown in Figure 4.15.

Break Card

Figure 4.15. Break Card

Make Another Choice Card

When teaching this visual support to students, make sure that autistic learners understand that this is a *helpful* card. You are using this card to help them not get in trouble and to help them be successful. This simple two-sided card—which is an evidence-based practice—is subtly given to the student when they need redirection in the classroom, hallway, workplace, community, or home (see Figure 4.16).

Figure 4.16. Make Another Choice Card

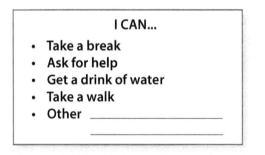

Graphic Organizers

Graphic organizers, such as semantic maps, Venn diagrams, outlines, and compare/contrast charts, provide visual, holistic representations of facts and concepts and their relationships within an organized framework. That is, these strategies arrange key terms to show their relationship to each other, presenting abstract or implicit information in a concrete manner. They are particularly useful with content-area material such as social studies, science, and so on, or tasks related to areas such as cooking, interviewing, and dating.

Graphic organizers often enhance the learning of autistics because:

- They are visual—a frequent area of strength.
- They are static; they remain consistent and constant.
- They allow for processing time; the individual can reflect on the material at his own pace.
- They are concrete and are more easily understood than a verbal-only presentation.

Figures 4.17, 4.18, and 4.19 provide examples of graphic organizers that (a) help an autistic employee understand the hidden meaning of what their boss said, (b) describe the water cycle, and (c) show the characteristics of a dog, respectively.

Figure 4.17. Graphic Organizer of Hidden Meaning of Supervisor's Comments

Friendly Things My Boss Says	Purely Friendly Comment	Comment with Hidden Meaning	Hidden Meaning
When you have time, please...		X	You have no choice but to do whatever you asked.
Good morning.	X		
It would be great if you could...		X	This is usually a directive, meaning you will do whatever it is.

From Myles, B. S., Endow, J., & Mayfield, M. (2013). The Hidden Curriculum of Getting and Keeping a Job. Navigating the Social Landscape of Employment. A Guide for Individuals with Autism and Other Social-Cognitive Challenges. *Arlington, TX: Future Horizons.*

Figure 4.18. Graphic Organizer That Explains the Water Cycle

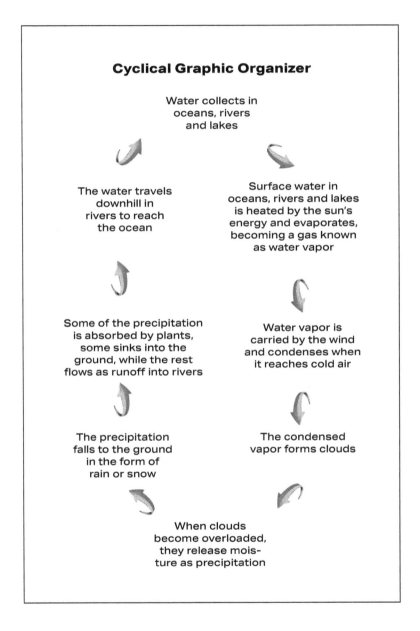

From Myles, B. S., & Adreon, D. (2001). Asperger Syndrome and Adolescence: Practical Solutions for School Success. Shawnee Mission, KS: AAPC Publishing.

Figure 4.19. Characteristics of a Dog

Obstacle Removal for the Support Person

One of the greatest obstacles to learning for everyone, including those with autism, is not having a positive relationship with a support person. James Comer (1995) said it best: "No significant learning can occur without a significant relationship." Thus, it is incumbent on the support person to ensure that this obstacle does not exist or, if it does, to remove it.

A meta-analysis of over 350,000 students revealed that the quality of early teacher-student relationships has a long-lasting impact (Cornelius-White, 2007). Ongoing positive teacher-student relationships in elementary school increase the likelihood that the learner will experience fewer episodes of negative behavior. In addition, students who have a positive relationship with teachers in kindergarten also have higher academic achievement, fewer behavioral problems, and better social skills through the eighth grade (cf. McCormick & O'Connor, 2015) and into high school (Kim, 2021). This clearly impacts the long-term trajectory of school and, eventually, employment.

Teachers who are in negative relationships with learners tend to feel frustrated, irritable, and angry. They often engage in educational bullying. Educational bullying occurs when adults who are members of the school staff use their power intentionally or unintentionally to cause students distress. Educators who bully tend to yell, make snide or sarcastic comments, and use harsh punitive control to manage behavior (Gusfre, Stoon, & Fandrem, 2022). These teachers often describe themselves as "struggling" or "in constant conflict" and describe students as "exhausting" or "leaving them feeling drained and burned out" (Rimm-Kaufman et al., 2002). Students in the classroom of such teachers not only miss out on the benefits of academic and social improvement but are also rejected, victimized, and bullied by classmates who model the inappropriate teacher behavior (Gusfre et al., 2022).

Learners who experience a positive relationship with support providers experience great advantages. Cornelius-White identified positive adult behaviors as well as associated learner outcomes (see Table 4.8).

Table 4.8. Teacher Relationships and Student/Classroom Outcomes

Adult Behaviors That Indicate a Positive Relationship with Learners	Learner Outcomes
• Engages in little conflict	• Has better social skills
• Is supportive of learner needs	• Accepts peers
• Is empathetic	• Develops social connections
• Supports independent and interdependent functioning	• Follow rules
• Decreases dependence	• Has higher academic performance
• Is trustworthy	• Is academically resilient
• Is positive	• Attends school regularly
• Feels close to learners	• Is self-directed
• Accepts learner ideas	• Participates in class
• Praises/reinforces	• Rates self as satisfied in school
• Accepts learner's feelings	• Is less likely to drop out of school
• Is sensitive to individual differences	• Is cooperative
• Involves learners in decision-making	• Has better mental health
• Is warm	• Explores options for higher education
• Is respectful	• Has good self-esteem/self-concept
• Encourages higher-level thinking	• Adjusts better to school academically and socially
• Is responsive to learner developmental, social, and personal needs	• Is motivated
	• Is less likely to be lonely
• Promotes student success	• Likes school
• Is genuine	• Shows self-control
	• Exhibits less defiant behavior/ aggression

Adapted from Cornelius-White, J. (2007). Learner-centered teacher-student relationships are effective: A meta-analysis. Review of Educational Research, *77(1), 113–143.*

How important are teacher-student relationships for autistic learners on the spectrum? VERY! Support personnel set the stage for student social success. Autistic students who have a positive relationship with their teachers have a higher level of social inclusion, have more peer relationships, and experience fewer behavior problems (Bolourian et al., 2021).

Summary

Helping autistic individuals to increase and enhance self-awareness, self-calming, and self-management requires a multifaceted approach. This includes instruction related to social, behavior, and academic skills; help in interpreting the environment; coaching to help use existing skills; and removing obstacles to ensure that individual needs are met. By using strategies in this chapter, autistic individuals will be better able to communicate their wants and needs and understand the often-challenging world. Similarly, support persons will become more effective and understanding. This is likely to result in fewer meltdowns. And, as a result, autistic individuals will be one step closer to their limitless potential!

━━ BIBLIOGRAPHY ━━

Albert, Linda. *A Teacher's Guide to Cooperative Discipline: How to Manage Your Classroom and Promote Self-Esteem*. Minnesota: American Guidance Service, 1989.

Diagnostic and Statistical Manual of Mental Disorders (Dsm-5(r)). 2013. 5ᵗʰ ed. American Psychiatric Publishing.

Armitano-Lago, Cortney, Hunter J. Bennett, and Justin A. Haegele. "Lower Limb Proprioception and Strength Differences between Adolescents with Autism Spectrum Disorder and Neurotypical Controls." *Perceptual and Motor Skills* 128, no. 5 (2021): 2132–47. https://doi.org/10.1177/00315125211036418

Arwood, Ellen L., and Mabel M. Brown. *A Guide to Cartooning and Flowcharting: See the Ideas*. Oregon: Apricot Inc., 1999.

Arwood, Ellen L., Mabel M. Brown, M.M., and Kaulitz, Carole. *Pro-social Language: A Way to Think about Behavior*. Oregon: Apricot Inc., 2015.

Aspy, Ruth, and Barry G. Grossman. *Underlying Characteristics Checklist: High Functioning*. Texas: The Ziggurat Group, 2022.

Aspy, Ruth, and Barry G. Grossman. *Underlying Characteristics Checklist: Classic*. Texas: The Ziggurat Group, 2022.

Aspy, Ruth, and Barry G. Grossman. *Underlying Characteristics Checklist: Early Intervention*. Texas: The Ziggurat Group, 2022.

Aspy, Ruth, and Barry G. Grossman. *Underlying Characteristics Checklist: Self-Report Adolescent*. Texas: The Ziggurat Group, 2022.

Aspy, Ruth, and Barry G. Grossman. *Underlying Characteristics Checklist: Self-Report Adult*. Texas: The Ziggurat Group, 2022.

Aspy, Ruth, and Barry G. Grossman. *The Ziggurat Model: A Framework for Designing Comprehensive Strategies and Supports for Autistic Individuals Release 2.1.* Texas: The Ziggurat Group, 2022.

Ruth Aspy, Barry G. Grossman, Brenda Smith Myles, and Shawn A. Henry. *FBA to Z: Functional Behavior Assessment and Intervention Plans for Individuals With ASD.* Texas: The Ziggurat Group, 2016.

Baker, Jed. *Social Skills Training for Children and Adolescents with Autism and Other Social-Communication Differences, 20th Anniversary Edition.* Texas: Future Horizons, 2023.

Baumeister, Sarah, Carolin Moessnang, Nico Bast, Sarah Hohmann, Pascal Aggensteiner, Anna Kaiser, Julian Tillmann, et al. "Processing of Social and Monetary Rewards in Autism Spectrum Disorders." *The British Journal of Psychiatry* 222, no. 3 (2023): 100–111. https://doi.org/10.1192/bjp.2022.157

Beck, Mitchell. "Understanding and Managing the Acting-Out Child." *The Pointer* 29, no. 2 (1985): 27-29.

Bellini, Scott. *Building Social Relationships 2: A Systematic Approach to Teaching Social Interaction Skills to Children and Adolescents on the Autism Spectrum.* Shawnee Mission, KS: AAPC Publishing 2016.

Bolourian, Yasamin, Ainsley Losh, Narmene Hamsho, Abbey Eisenhower, and Jan Blacher. "General Education Teachers' Perceptions of Autism, Inclusive Practices, and Relationship Building Strategies." *Journal of Autism and Developmental Disorders* 52, no. 9 (2021): 3977–90. https://doi.org/10.1007/s10803-021-05266-4

Boudjarane, Mohamed A., Marine Grandgeorge, Rémi Marianowski, Laurent Misery, and Éric Lemonnier. "Perception of Odors and Tastes in Autism Spectrum Disorders: A Systematic Review of Assessments." *Autism Research* 10, no. 6 (2017): 1045–57. https://doi.org/10.1002/aur.1760

Buron, Kari. D., and Mitzi Curtis, M. *The Incredible 5-Point Scale 2nd Edition Revised.* Minnesota: 5 Point Scale Publishing, 2022.

Bury, Simon M., Darren Hedley, Mirko Uljarević, and Eynat Gal. "The Autism Advantage at Work: A Critical and Systematic Review of Current Evidence." *Research in Developmental Disabilities* 105 (2020): 103750. https://doi.org/10.1016/j.ridd.2020.103750

Carey, Timothy A., and W. Thomas Bourbon. "Countercontrol: New Look at Some Old Problems." *Intervention in School and Clinic* 40, no. 1 (2004): 3–9. https://doi.org/10.1177/10534512040400010101

Chung, Seungwon, and Jung-Woo Son. "Visual Perception in Autism Spectrum Disorder: A Review of Neuroimaging Studies." *Journal of the Korean Academy of Child and Adolescent Psychiatry* 31, no. 3 (2020): 105–20. https://doi.org/10.5765/jkacap.200018

Clark, Megan, and Dawn Adams. "Parent-Reported Barriers and Enablers of Strengths in Their Children with Autism." *Journal of Child and Family Studies* 29, no. 9 (2020): 2402–15. https://doi.org/10.1007/s10826-020-01741-1

Comer, James. "Relationships," (lecture, Education Service Center, Region IV, Houston, Texas, 1995).

Cornelius-White, Jeffrey. "Learner-Centered Teacher-Student Relationships Are Effective: A Meta-Analysis." *Review of Educational Research* 77, no. 1 (2007): 113–43. https://doi.org/10.3102/003465430298563.

DeBar, Ruth M., Courtney L. Kane, and Jessica L. Amador. 3033. "Video Modeling Instruction for Individuals with Autism Spectrum Disorder." In *Handbook of Applied Behavior Analysis Interventions for Autism: Integrating Research into Practice*, 227–50. Cham, Switzerland: Springer International Publishing.

Dell'Osso, L., B. Carpita, D. Muti, V. Morelli, G. Salarpi, A. Salerni, J. Scotto, et al. "Mood Symptoms and Suicidality across the Autism Spectrum." *Comprehensive Psychiatry* 91 (2019): 34–38. https://doi.org/10.1016/j.comppsych.2019.03.004.

Egarr, Rachael, and Catherine Storey. "Model Teachers or Model Students? A Comparison of Video Modelling Interventions for Improving Reading

Fluency and Comprehension in Children with Autism." *Journal of Autism and Developmental Disorders* 52, no. 8 (2021): 3366–82. https://doi.org/10.1007/s10803-021-05217-z.

Espenhahn, Svenja, Kate J. Godfrey, Sakshi Kaur, Carly McMorris, Kara Murias, Mark Tommerdahl, Signe Bray, and Ashley D. Harris. "Atypical Tactile Perception in Early Childhood Autism." *Journal of Autism and Developmental Disorders*, 2022. https://doi.org/10.1007/s10803-022-05570-7.

Familydoctor.org. 2023. "Sensory Processing Disorder (SPD)" June 8, 2023. https://familydoctor.org/condition/sensory-processing-disorder-spd/.

Gagnon, Elisa, and Myles, Brenda Smith. *The Power Card Strategy 2.0: Using Special Interests to Motivate Children and Youth with Autism Spectrum Disorder.* Kansas: AAPC Publishing 2016.

Ghaziuddin, Neera, Laura Andersen, and Mohammad Ghaziuddin. "Catatonia in Patients with Autism Spectrum Disorder." *Psychiatric Clinics of North America* 44, no. 1 (2021): 11–22. https://doi.org/10.1016/j.psc.2020.11.002

Grandin, T. "Learning Social Rules," *Autism Asperger's Digest*, January/February 2005.

Gray, Carol. (1994). *Comic Strip Conversations*™. Texas: Future Horizons, 1994.

Gray, Carol. *The New Social Story*™ *Book, Revised and Expanded 15th Anniversary Edition: Over 150 Social Stories That Teach Everyday Skills to Children and Adults with Autism and Their Peers.* Texas: Future Horizons, 2016.

Green, Shulamite A., Leanna Hernandez, Nim Tottenham, Kate Krasileva, Susan Y. Bookheimer, and Mirella Dapretto. "Neurobiology of sensory overresponsivity in youth with autism spectrum disorders." *JAMA Psychiatry* 72, no. 8 (2015): 778-786.

Gusfre, Kari Stamland, Janne Støen, and Hildegunn Fandrem. "Bullying by Teachers towards Students—a Scoping Review." *International Journal of Bullying Prevention*, 2022. https://doi.org/10.1007/s42380-022-00131-z

Herrero, Jorge Fernández, and Gonzalo Lorenzo. "An Immersive Virtual Reality Educational Intervention on People with Autism Spectrum Disorders (ASD) for the Development of Communication Skills and Problem Solving." *Education and Information Technologies* 25, no. 3 (2019): 1689–1722. https://doi.org/10.1007/s10639-019-10050-0

Kilroy, Emily, Lisa Aziz-Zadeh, and Sharon Cermak. "Ayres Theories of Autism and Sensory Integration Revisited: What Contemporary Neuroscience Has to Say." *Brain Sciences* 9, no. 3 (2019): 68. https://doi.org/10.3390/brainsci9030068

Kim, Jinho. "The Quality of Social Relationships in Schools and Adult Health: Differential Effects of Student–Student versus Student–Teacher Relationships." *School Psychology* 36, no. 1 (2021): 6–16. https://doi.org/10.1037/spq0000373

Leaf, Justin B., Julia L. Ferguson, Joseph H. Cihon, Christine M. Milne, Ronald Leaf, and John McEachin. "A Critical Review of Social Narratives." *Journal of Developmental and Physical Disabilities* 32, no. 2 (2019): 241–56. https://doi.org/10.1007/s10882-019-09692-2

LaVoie, Rick. "Last One Picked: First One Picked On." YouTube video. 1:14:34, 1994. https://www.youtube.com/watch?v=TyaHlOYtkI4

Lewis, Laura Foran, and Kailey Stevens. "The lived experience of meltdowns for autistic adults." *Autism* (2023): 13623613221145783.

Long, Nicholas J., William C. Morse, and Ruth Newman. *Conflict in the Classroom: The Educational Children with Problems (3rd ed.)*. California: Wadsworth, 1976.

Mahler, Kelly. *The Interoception Curriculum: A Step-by-Step Guide to Developing Mindful Self-Regulation*. Pennsylvania: Kelly Mahler, 2019.

Mahler, Kelly, Kerri Hample, Claudia Jones, Joseph Sensenig, Phoebe Thomasco, and Claudia Hilton. "Impact of an Interoception-Based Program on Emotion Regulation in Autistic Children." *Occupational Therapy International 2022* (2022): 1–7. https://doi.org/10.1155/2022/9328967

Marko, Mollie K., Deana Crocetti, Thomas Hulst, Opher Donchin, Reza Shadmehr, and Stewart H. Mostofsky. "Behavioural and Neural Basis of Anomalous Motor Learning in Children with Autism." *Brain* 138, no. 3 (2015): 784–97. https://doi.org/10.1093/brain/awu394

Mataya, Kerry, Ruth Aspy, and Hollis Shaffer, H. *Talk with Me: A Step-by-Step Conversation Framework for Teaching Conversational Balance and Fluency.* Texas: Future Horizons, 2017.

Mataya, Kerry, and Penny Owens. *Successful Problem-Solving for High-Functioning Students with Autism Spectrum Disorder.* Texas: Future Horizons, 2013.

McAfee, Jeanette. *Navigating the Social World: A Curriculum for Individuals with Asperger's Syndrome, High Functioning Autism, and Related Disorders.* Texas: Future Horizons, 2013.

McCormick, Meghan P., and Erin E. O'Connor. 2015. "Teacher–Child Relationship Quality and Academic Achievement in Elementary School: Does Gender Matter?" *Journal of Educational Psychology* 107 (2): 502–516. https://doi.org/10.1037/a0037457

Murray, Christopher, and Kimber Malmgren. "Implementing a Teacher–Student Relationship Program in a High-Poverty Urban School: Effects on Social, Emotional, and Academic Adjustment and Lessons Learned." *Journal of School Psychology* 43, no. 2 (2005): 137–52. https://doi.org/10.1016/j.jsp.2005.01.003

Myles, Brenda Smith, and Diane Adreon. *Asperger Syndrome and Adolescence: Practical Solutions for School Success.* Kansas: AAPC Publishing, 2001.

Myles, Brenda Smith, Judy Endow, and Malcom Mayfield, M. (2013). *The Hidden Curriculum of Getting and Keeping a Job: Navigating the Social Landscape of Employment. A Guide for Individuals with Autism Spectrum Disorders and Other Social-Cognitive Challenges.* Texas: Future Horizons, 2013.

Myles, Brenda Smith, & Richard L. Simpson, R. L. The Aggression Cycle and Teacher Strategies for Prevention/Intervention. *The Prevention Researcher*, 6 no. 2 (1999), 9¬–11.

Myles, Brenda Smith, Melissa Trautman, and Ronda L. Schelvan. (2013). *The Hidden Curriculum: Practical Solutions for Understanding Unstated Rules in Social Situations (2nd ed.).* Texas: Future Horizons, 2013.

Ni, Hsing-Chang, Hsiang-Yuan Lin, Yu-Chieh Chen, Wen-Yih Isaac Tseng, and Susan Shur-Fen Gau. "Boys with Autism Spectrum Disorder Have Distinct Cortical Folding Patterns Underpinning Impaired Self-Regulation: A Surface-Based Morphometry Study." *Brain Imaging and Behavior* 14, no. 6 (2019): 2464–76. https://doi.org/10.1007/s11682-019-00199-0

Ni, Hsing-Chang, Hsiang-Yuan Lin, Yu-Chieh Chen, Wen-Yih Isaac Tseng, and Susan Shur-Fen Gau. "Boys with Autism Spectrum Disorder Have Distinct Cortical Folding Patterns Underpinning Impaired Self-Regulation: A Surface-Based Morphometry Study." *Brain Imaging and Behavior* 14, no. 6 (2019): 2464–76. https://doi.org/10.1007/s11682-019-00199-0

"Kit for Kids: OAR." Organization for Autism Research, April 7, 2023. https://researchautism.org/educators/kit-for-kids/#whats-up-with-nick-booklets

Phung, Jasmine, Melanie Penner, Clémentine Pirlot, and Christie Welch. "What I Wish You Knew: Insights on Burnout, Inertia, Meltdown, and Shutdown from Autistic Youth." *Frontiers in Psychology* 12 (2021). https://doi.org/10.3389/fpsyg.2021.741421

Pingale, Vidya, Tina Fletcher, and Catherine Candler. "The Effects of Sensory Diets on Children's Classroom Behaviors." *Journal of Occupational Therapy*, Schools, & Early Intervention 12, no. 2 (2019): 225–38. https://doi.org/10.1080/19411243.2019.1592054

Prince, Julia, Matt Tincani, and Art Dowdy. "Effects of the Power Card Strategy on Social Commenting of Children with Autism during Gameplay: Strength-Based Intervention." *Journal of Positive Behavior Interventions*, 2023, 109830072311588. https://doi.org/10.1177/10983007231158816

Rahn, Naomi L., Christan Grygas Coogle, Alexajo Hanna, and Traysha Lewellen. "Evidence-Based Practices to Reduce Challenging Behaviors of Young Children with Autism." *Young Exceptional Children* 20, no. 4 (2015): 166–78. https://doi.org/10.1177/1096250615598816

Richey, J. Anthony, Cara R. Damiano, Antoinette Sabatino, Alison Rittenberg, Chris Petty, Josh Bizzell, James Voyvodic, et al. "Neural Mechanisms of Emotion Regulation in Autism Spectrum Disorder." *Journal of Autism and Developmental Disorders* 45, no. 11 (2015): 3409–23. https://doi.org/10.1007/s10803-015-2359-z

Rimm-Kaufman, Sara E, Diane M Early, Martha J Cox, Gitanjali Saluja, Robert C Pianta, Robert H Bradley, and Chris Payne. "Early Behavioral Attributes and Teachers' Sensitivity as Predictors of Competent Behavior in the Kindergarten Classroom." *Journal of Applied Developmental Psychology* 23, no. 4 (2002): 451–70. https://doi.org/10.1016/s0193-3973(02)00128-4

Rotschafer, Sarah Elizabeth. "Auditory Discrimination in Autism Spectrum Disorder." *Frontiers in Neuroscience* 15 (2021). https://doi.org/10.3389/fnins.2021.651209

Roux, Anne, Jessica Rast, Julianna Rava, Kristy Anderson, and Paul Shattuck. *National Autism Indicators Report: Transition into Young Adulthood. Life Course Outcomes Research Program*, AJ Drexel Autism Institute, Drexel University, 2015.

Rowland, David. "A Need to Redefine Autism: A Review." Recent Developments in *Medicine and Medical Research* Vol. 5, 2021, 67–74. https://doi.org/10.9734/bpi/rdmmr/v5/14008d

Samuel, M. "Are You a Problem Solver or an Obstacle Remover?" *Forbes*, July 11, 2019.

Schopler, Eric. "Behavioral priorities for autism and related developmental disorders." *Behavioral Issues in Autism* (1994): 55¬–77.

Sinha, Pawan, Margaret M. Kjelgaard, Tapan K. Gandhi, Kleovoulos Tsourides, Annie L. Cardinaux, Dimitrios Pantazis, Sidney P. Diamond, and Richard M. Held. "Autism as a disorder of prediction." *Proceedings of the National Academy of Sciences* 111, no. 42 (2014): 15220–15225.

Soulières, Isabelle, Michelle Dawson, Fabienne Samson, Elise B. Barbeau, Chérif P. Sahyoun, Gary E. Strangman, Thomas A. Zeffiro, and Laurent

Mottron. "Enhanced Visual Processing Contributes to Matrix Reasoning in Autism." *Human Brain Mapping* 30, no. 12 (2009): 4082–4107. https://doi.org/10.1002/hbm.20831

Vaquerizo-Serrano, J., G. Salazar De Pablo, J. Singh, and P. Santosh. "Catatonia in Autism Spectrum Disorders: A Systematic Review and Meta-Analysis." *European Psychiatry* 65, no. 1 (2021). https://doi.org/10.1192/j.eurpsy.2021.2259

Vermeulen, Peter. *Autism and the Predictive Brain: Absolute Thinking in a Relative World*. England: Routledge, 2023.

Vermeulen, Peter. *Autism as Context Blindness*. Texas: Future Horizons, 2012.

Watkins, Laci, Katherine Ledbetter-Cho, Mark O'Reilly, Lucy Barnard-Brak, and Pau Garcia-Grau. "Interventions for Students with Autism in Inclusive Settings: A Best-Evidence Synthesis and Meta-Analysis." *Psychological Bulletin* 145, no. 5 (2019): 490–507. https://doi.org/10.1037/bul0000190

Wolfberg, Pamela. J. *Peer Play and the Autism Spectrum: The Art of Guiding Children's Socialization and Imagination*. Kansas: AAPC Publishing, 2003.

About the Author

Brenda Smith Myles Ph.D., formerly a professor in the Department of Special Education at the University of Kansas, is the recipient of the Autism Society of America's Outstanding Professional Award, the Princeton Fellowship Award, The Global and Regional Asperger Syndrome (GRASP) Divine Neurotypical Award, American Academy of Pediatrics Autism Champion, and two-time recipient of the Council for Exceptional Children Burton Blatt Humanitarian Award. She served as the editor of the journal Intervention in School and Clinic and has been a member of the editorial board of several journals. Brenda has made over 3000 presentations all over the world and written more than 300 articles and books on autism.

Printed in the USA
CPSIA information can be obtained
at www.ICGtesting.com
JSHW010959230424
E13476300001B/1